MYSTERY

BABYLON
THE GREAT,

THE MOTHER OF HARLOTS
AND ABOMINATIONS OF
THE EARTH

Harold T. Bolieu

Aspect Books

PRINTED IN
THE UNITED STATES OF AMERICA

All Scripture references are taken from the Authorized King James Bible. Some textual emphasis is supplied by the author.

No matter what your religious affiliation may be, I truly believe (whether you profess to be a Christian or not) that every person should read this study. If, however, someone should advise you not to read the information contained herein, then you must ask yourself, "What could possibly be written on these pages that they do not want me to read? What are they afraid I might find out?"

2010 11 12 13 14 · 5 4 3 2 1

End Harvest Ministries
P.O. Box 49
Poteet, Texas 78065

Published by

End Harvest Ministries

CONTENTS

KEYS TO UNDERSTANDING PROPHETIC SYMBOLS

Although a few of these will be repeated throughout the study, here is the main list:

1. A prophetic day equals one full year according to Numbers 14:34, which states, "After the number of the days in which ye searched the land, even forty days, each day for a year, shall ye bear your iniquities, even forty years, and ye shall know my breach of promise." And in Ezekiel 4:4-6 it states, "Lie thou also upon thy left side, and lay the iniquity of the house of Israel upon it: according to the number of the days that thou shalt lie upon it thou shalt bear their iniquity. For I have laid upon thee the years of their iniquity, according to the number of the days, three hundred and ninety days: so shalt thou bear the iniquity of the house of Israel. And when thou hast accomplished them, lie again on thy right side, and thou shalt bear the iniquity of the house of Judah forty days: I have appointed thee each day for a year."

2. It is also commonly taught that we are to translate the last nine words of Daniel 7:25, "A time and times and the dividing of time," as, "one year, two years, and a half of a year." Which, going by the Jewish calendar of twelve months with thirty day months, equates to the following: 360 days = 1 year, 720 days = 2 years, and 180 days = ½ year, which equals 1260 years, the same amount of days of Daniel 7:25.

3. Beast and animals represent kingdoms and powers according to Daniel 7:17 and 23, which states, "These great beast, which are four, are four kings, which shall arise out of the earth. . . . Thus he said, The fourth beast shall be the fourth kingdom upon earth, which shall be diverse from all kingdoms, and shall devour the whole earth, and shall tread it down, and break it in pieces."

4. Horns represent kings according to Daniel 7:24, which states, "And the ten horns out of this kingdom are ten kings that shall arise: and another shall rise after them; and he shall be diverse from the first, and he shall subdue [overthrow, overcome] three kings."

5. Water represents peoples, multitudes, nations, and tongues, according to Revelation 17:15, which reads "And he saith unto me, The waters which thou sawest, where the whore sitteth, are peoples, and multitudes, and nations, and tongues."

6. Wind represents war, strife, and turmoil according to Jeremiah 25:32, where we read, "Thus saith the LORD of hosts, Behold, evil shall go forth from nation to nation, and a great whirlwind shall be raised up from the coasts of the earth." Additionally, Jeremiah 49:36-37 states, "And upon Elam will I bring the four winds from the four quarters of heaven, and will scatter them toward all those winds; and there shall be no nation whither the outcasts of Elam shall not come. For I will cause Elam to be dismayed before their enemies, and before them that seek their life: and I will bring evil upon them, even my fierce anger, saith the LORD; and I will send the sword after them, till I have consumed them."

7. A pure woman (a virgin) represents a pure church according to Jeremiah 6:2: "I have likened the daughter

of Zion to a comely and delicate woman." Furthermore, 2 Corinthians 11:2 reads, "For I am jealous over you with godly jealousy: for I have espoused you to one husband, that I may present you as a chaste virgin to Christ." See also Hosea 2:19-20 and Isaiah 62:4-5.

8. An impure woman (a harlot) represents an apostate church according to Revelation 18:2-10. Verse 7 states, "How much she hath glorified herself, and lived deliciously, so much torment and sorrow give her: for she saith in her heart, I sit a queen, and am no widow, and shall see no sorrow." Read also Isaiah 47:1-15.

9. The harvest points to the second coming of our Lord Jesus Christ (as in the end of the world) according to Matthew 13:39, which states, "The enemy that sowed them is the devil; the harvest is the end of the world; and the reapers are the angels." Read also Revelation 14:14-15.

10. Wheat represents God's elect while tares represent those outside God's will as shown in Matthew 13:24-30, but God says of these two groups, "Let both grow together until the harvest: and in the time of harvest I will say to the reapers, Gather ye together first the tares, and bind them in bundles to burn them: but gather the wheat into my barn" (verse 30). Read also Matthew 3:12.

11. A Lamb, a Rock, The Stone Cut Without Hands, or a Corner Stone represents our Lord Jesus Christ. We are shown this in numerous passages. "Now therefore ye are no more strangers and foreigners, but fellow citizens with the saints, and of the household of God; And are built upon the foundation of the apostles and prophets, Jesus Christ himself being the chief corner stone" (Ephesians 2:19-20). "And did all drink the

same spiritual drink: for they drank of that spiritual Rock that followed them: and that Rock was Christ" (1 Corinthians 10:4). "Forasmuch as thou sawest that the stone was cut out of the mountain without hands, and that it brake in pieces the iron, the brass, the clay, the silver, and the gold; the great God hath made known to the king what shall come to pass hereafter: and the dream is certain, and the interpretation thereof sure" (Daniel 2:45). "The next day John seeth Jesus coming unto him, and saith, Behold the Lamb of God, which taketh away the sin of the world" (John 1:29). See also Daniel 2:34 and John 1:36.

12. Truth is also referred to as a rock. Read Matthew 16:18, which states, "And I say also unto you, That thou art Peter, and upon this rock I will build my church: and the gates of hell shall not prevail against it." This verse refers us to another verse that I have already shown: Ephesians 2:20.

13. The dragon refers to Satan, the devil, according to Revelation 12:9: "And the great dragon was cast out, that old serpent, called the Devil, and Satan, which deceiveth the whole world: he was cast out into the earth, and his angels were cast out with him."

14. The color white denotes purity and/or holiness, while the colors red or scarlet denote sin according to Isaiah 1:18: "Come now, and let us reason together, saith the LORD: though your sins be as scarlet, they shall be as white as snow; though they be red like crimson, they shall be as wool."

15. Beast and/or beast heads represent kings and kingdoms according to Daniel 7 and Revelation 17:9-10, while wings on the beast represent swiftness of movement, according to Revelation 12:14. "After this I beheld, and

lo another, like a leopard, which had upon the back of it four wings of a fowl; the beast has also four heads; and dominion was given to it" (Daniel 7:6). "Thus he said, The fourth beast shall be the fourth kingdom upon earth, which shall be diverse from all kingdoms, and shall devour the whole earth, and shall tread it down, and break it in pieces" (Daniel 7:23). "And to the woman were given two wings of a great eagle, that she might fly into the wilderness, into her place, where she is nourished for a time, and times, and half a time, from the face of the serpent" (Revelation 12:14).

GOD'S WARNINGS AND PROMISES

"And I heard another voice from heaven, saying, Come out of her, my people, that ye be not partakers of her sins, and that ye receive not of her plagues."

Revelation 18:4

"And no marvel; for Satan himself is transformed into an angel of light. Therefore it is no great thing if his ministers also be transformed as the ministers of righteousness; whose end shall be according to their works."

2 Corinthians 11:14-15

"Henceforth I call you not servants; for the servants knoweth not what his lord doeth: but I have called you friends; for all things that I have heard of my Father I have made known to you."

John 15:15

This is my prayer for you, the reader of this book:

"Heavenly Father, I pray that Your Holy Spirit come near to guide each reader through this study, and help them not only understand but also receive and accept Your truths as You have presented them to us in Your Holy Word. Amen."

FOREWORD AND PURPOSE

This study contains "Bible facts" that are coupled with historical events and are in response to a few articles that have appeared in some of the more popular news magazines which I have included in full at the back of this book.

The first article, which is titled "Book claims pope is the devil's ally," refers to the everyday working class adult as "the Joe Six Packs of the world." It presents the idea that the average person is apparently unable to think or decide what they will believe for themselves, therefore, they must be "instructed as children" what they should or should not believe.

The second, "Vatican Thinking Evolves," has a picture of Pope John Paul II and beneath it the caption reads "John Paul does not interpret the Bible literally."

This is why I explain to everyone I speak with, "How you receive this information depends on how you receive the Bible itself." In other words, "Do you believe the Bible to be the inspired Word of God, 'literally,' as I do or not? By literally, I mean, it states in Genesis 1:1 and 2:3 that God created the heavens and the earth and everything that is either on or in them in six days. And God rested on and blessed and sanctified the seventh day. If you do not believe this, then you would probably be better off if you laid this book aside right now and didn't read another word.

You see, my friend, there can be no middle ground. Jesus Himself states in Revelation 3:15-16: "I know thy works, that thou art neither cold nor hot: I would rather thou wert cold or hot. So then because thou art lukewarm, and neither cold nor hot, I will spue thee out of my mouth."

Then I present "The Pope and Darwin" with a picture of Pope John Paul, and in bold letters to the right side is printed "The Pope Says We May Descend From Monkeys." When I read this one, it really troubled me. But then I remembered where we are (time wise) in Bible prophecy.

Next you will find "No Forgiveness Directly From God, Pope Says." After reading this article, one must ask themselves, "Why in the world would the pope, the 'head' of the Roman Catholic Church system, the largest and richest religious system in the world, make such off-the-wall statements? What could be behind this supposed change of direction? By change of direction, I mean, isn't the pope supposed to be leading people to a clearer understanding of God and His Holy Word? Instead, it seems as though he is soliciting worship for himself and his clergy—as if he were a god, as all past popes have claimed, by the way, back through the long ages of history.

And, if this were not enough, we have on the following page "Disregarding Sunday as a day of rest may hurt us culturally." This is an article taken from a Lutheran magazine which asks the question "Is killing Sunday killing us?" Also, included in this article is a quote that reads, "Movement to reclaim Sabbath grows," which is a newspaper headline of a story about the Lord's Day Alliance, which is an interdenominational group that claims it is trying to protect the Sabbath day. The group further claims that the "Christian Sabbath Day" is Sunday—of which, you will see for yourselves is not the truth. But, they have the right to believe whatever they want, although it is not a biblical teaching. The same is true concerning many of the teachings they claim are biblical but are not. And this, my dear friend, is one of the main reasons I am presenting this information to you.

The second reason I am presenting this information to you is that I am commanded through Scripture to do so; thereby, making you aware of certain events that have already taken place and others which are soon to occur in the very near future.

There are a couple of points I want to make before we begin this study. This study is in no way an attempt, nor is it intended, to convert you to my way of thinking. In fact, I ask that you not believe anything that is written hereafter until you have not only checked out but also proven this information for yourselves. And, you must not allow this study or anything anyone has told you in the past or will tell you in the future, myself included, to sway your decision concerning how you perceive God's Holy Word. Be sure. Prove everything. No matter how sincere their efforts or mine may seem, in the end only your decision will be taken into consideration.

This is not a "new revelation" nor is it some "new found gospel." Personally, I believe what you are about to read is the "same gospel" that was not only taught to but proclaimed by the first twelve, excluding Judas Iscariot, but including Stephen, the first man martyred for preaching the gospel of Jesus Christ, which occurred in AD 33. (Read Acts 7.)

I am adding the following disclaimer, because I have been told by many Catholics, and some Protestants, that this work is unacceptable because I have not the authority, background, or credentials to write such a scandalous thing as this. Nor has this work been sanctioned by the so-called "church fathers"; therefore, I am a heretic according to the "teachings and traditions" of approximately 95 percent of all priests, preachers, and Bible teachers. However, most of those "church traditions" are even today held above the Bible's authority.

So here is my disclaimer. I alone take full responsibility for all information contained throughout this book, which covers not only the identification of the antichrist but also the beast, the mark of the beast, the image of the beast, and information about where the beast has ruled from for almost two thousand years. I know there will be those who will attempt to prove not only these truths false but will attempt to discredit the men and women who discovered and taught many of these same truths so many years ago.

Men and women who I believe had to have been chosen by God to lead His people from the "spiritual darkness" of the middle ages back to the truth of His Holy Word. Men and women who loved God and His truths so much that they went against this cruel, sadistic, paganistic, dictatorial church system, whose leaders were nothing short of dictators themselves. Many of those men and women literally laid down their lives in order to turn the minds and hearts of the common people, the "Joe Six Packs" or "separated brethren" as we are referred to today by the Catholic fathers, back to God's true gospel—people such as John Wyckliff, John Huss, John Calvin, William Tyndal, Martin Luther, and Hugh Latimer to name only a few.

But try as they may, I assure you that those who disagree with this book cannot disprove any of the facts that I am about to show you. Not from any of the many world history books and certainly not from the Bible. They may try to show proofs from other books which they or others from their beliefs have written. And of this, I must caution you; have them prove these things wrong from the King James Version Bible *only*.

I stress this because anyone can put a few obscure verses together and make them mean anything "they" want them to. After all, as long as they do not have to show any proof of their story being true, what do they care? And this is the reason those preachers place most of the prophetic events in the distant future rather than in the past where they belong. But, in their attempt to disprove these things, many will come to accept them as the truths they are simply through the investigation of the facts I am going to show you. I must say, many of those preachers and teachers are truly good men and women who can see God's truths being revealed but would rather play it safe than attempt to go against the main stream religions of today.

This is how so many of the teachings and traditions of the Catholic Church have been included in the Protestant Church services. And these things have been going on for so long that Protestants of today have again forgotten what a costly price was paid for their salvation.

But I challenge both those preachers and you to go to the library and check out *Foxe's Book of Martyrs*, written by John Fox, or many of the history books that were written of that time in world history that would be between the years AD 538 through AD 1798. It may seem as though I am a hateful person for showing and telling you some of the things you are about to read, but I wonder what the people thought of Jesus' teachings. I mean, after all, they killed Him.

Some of the following information will seem as though it is being repeated over and over, but it is only because the same information is repeated several times throughout Scripture. God wanted to be sure that the people who diligently search His Word would find these truths. Most people do not know that God instructs us on how we are to study the Bible. Let me show you what I mean. In Isaiah 28:9-10 we read, "Whom shall he teach knowledge? and whom shall he make to understand doctrine? them that are weaned from the milk, and drawn from the breasts. For precept must be upon precept, precept upon precept; line upon line, line upon line; here a little, and there a little."

So, do not be fooled. When anyone tries to talk about the Bible with you, first, ask them where whatever they are talking about can be found if you do not already know. Second, when you get away from whomever it is you are talking with, check it out for yourself.

This same idea is what God's Word is referring to in Jeremiah 6:10, which reads, "To whom shall I speak, and give warning, that they may hear? behold, their ear is uncircumcised, and they cannot hearken: behold, the word of the LORD is unto them a reproach; they have no delight in it." And to this may I say, the reason they have no delight in it is because God's Word goes against everything they have ever been taught concerning God and His Holy Word. Read also Acts 7:51.

We also find in Matthew 13:10-13 the following words: "And the disciples came, and said unto him, Why speakest thou unto them in parables? He answered and said unto them, Because it is given unto you to know the mysteries of the kingdom of heaven, but to them it is not given. . . . Therefore speak I to them in parables: because they seeing see not; and hearing they hear not, neither do they understand."

As I tell most people, it may seem as though I am repeating myself at times, but I assure you it is not for my own inflated ego. The reason is so there will be no doubt as to what I am trying to convey to you.

CAUTION, WARNING, TAKE HEED, READER BEWARE

The information contained on the following pages is considered, by many, to be highly controversial and will probably change your view of everything you have ever been taught concerning God's Holy Word and all end-time events. So, I warn you to proceed with caution.

GOD'S SPECIFICATIONS

To begin, it is very important for us to understand that God has placed certain specifications in His Holy Word that we must compare all things to. If our ideas do not match 100 percent with what God is showing us, then we have either missed something or, because of our pride and not wanting to be wrong, we have not allowed God's Word to show us certain things.

For instance, when referring to the antichrist, there are many preachers and Bible teachers who claim it was Emperor Nero, Napoleon, Kaiser Wilhelm, or Hitler. There was even a man on the radio a while back who said he could prove, without a doubt, that the antichrist was Prince Charles. The reason he believed this was because on Prince Charles' coat of arms there are a few of the animals that are spoken of in the books of Daniel and Revelation. Supposedly, if you took Prince Charles' name and translated it into numbers, using two different languages, you would come out with 666. Now, while I do agree this fellow is on the right track, I must disagree with his findings.

I once even saw a Bible that contained an inscription at the bottom of the page referencing Revelation 13:18. The inscription stated that the number of the beast, which is 666, referred to Nero. The reason many claim this is because they suppose, as many preachers teach, the word "anti" only means against. But, if you check this out for yourselves, you will find that the word "anti" in the Greek language, which was the common language of Jesus' time, can actually be used in two different ways. When used one way, it does, in fact, mean against. But, when used the other way, it means in place of. Just as many preachers teach that somewhere in the near future everyone will be forced to have a triple 6 branded on their forehead or in their right hand. But, as you will see, 666 is only one of the many identifying clues we must use to find out who the antichrist really is. You will also see that no one else will receive this number. It is only "his" number; the number of "his" name. God's Holy Word tells us this in Revelation 13:17.

WHO AND WHERE IS THE ANTICHRIST?

Now, while all the aforementioned names are very good guesses, not one comes close to qualifying as the antichrist, simply because not one of those men comes close to matching the specifically detailed description given in God's Holy Word. After all, we can't just pull a name out of the air and because of the terrible things he may have done point to that person and say that had to be the antichrist.

Now, to begin with, it is a man we are looking for and it is also true that if we change the letters of his name into their numerical equations we would come away with the number 666. Not just anybody fits the entire criteria. There are many more matching cogs that have to be fitted into place before we can even hope to come close to identifying this man. For instance, Scripture tells us that this man has to be the head or leader of a worldwide religious/political system. And his teachings or practices must be contrary to what the teachings are of both the Old and New Testaments. His teachings and practices must somehow correspond with those of ancient Babylon. Also, it is an organization whose power increased as the Old Roman Empire's power was decreasing. So, with these things in mind, let's begin our search.

Let's begin with 2 Thessalonians 2:3-4, "Let no man deceive you by any means: for that day shall not come [referring to the second coming of our Lord Jesus Christ], except there come a falling away first [referring to falling away from the true gospel], and that man of sin be revealed, the son of perdition; who opposeth and exalteth himself above all that is called God, or that is worshipped; so that he as God sitteth in the temple of God, shewing himself that he is God."

Now, there are many out there who read the last section of this verse like this: So that he as *a* god, sitteth in the temple of God, shewing himself that he is *a* god. As you can see, by adding this one single letter "a," these people have completely changed not only the whole sentence but the whole prophecy. As you can also see for yourself, this is not at all what the verse is saying.

Now, as I said before, the reference given to the falling away can refer to nothing other than the falling away from the true gospel teachings of God's Holy Word and can refer to no other time in history than between the years AD 538 and AD 1798, a total of 1260 years—the same amount of time mentioned in Daniel 7:25, 12:7 and Revelation 11:2-3, 12:6, 12:14, and 13:5 referring to days and times. I know you may be a little confused at this point, but please keep reading; the fog will become a little clearer after this next section.

Take a look at Numbers 14:34, which reads, "After the number of the days in which ye searched the land, even forty days, each day for a year, shall ye bear your iniquities, even forty years, and ye shall know my breach of promise." (40 days = 40 years.)

Then, in Ezekiel 4:4-6 we read, "Lie thou also upon thy left side, and lay the iniquity of the house of Israel upon it: according to the number of the days that thou shalt lie upon it thou shalt bear their iniquity. For I have laid upon thee the years of their iniquity, according to the number of the days, three hundred and ninety days: so shalt thou bear the iniquity of the house of Israel. And when thou hast accomplished them, lie again on thy right side, and thou shalt bear the iniquity of the house of Judah forty days: I have appointed thee each day for a year." (Israel 390 days = 390 years; Judah 40 days = 40 years.)

Could anything have been made any clearer? We are instructed by God's Word that when we are studying prophecy that contains a timeline in days we are to change those days into years. The same is true with these 1260 days. In order for us to find and identify what we are looking for, we must change these 1260 days into 1260 years. Once we do this we are able to go to the history books and find exactly what we are looking for.

And this brings me back to what I mentioned before. If you will subtract AD 538 from AD 1798, you will come out with 1260 years (referring to the same timeframes I just spoke of). When studying the history of those days, we find out that it was forbidden by all the popes of the Roman Catholic Church, under penalty and pains of death, for anyone outside the priesthood of the Roman Catholic Church to read or have in their possession any part of the Bible—the Bible was a forbidden book!

I tell you my friend, in the history of the world there has never been another human being who not only claims he sits in the place of God as the mediator between God and man but further claims that only through him can mankind be saved. He also claims to be equal with God and be able to forgive the sins of mankind (even those of the dead), therefore, demanding to be worshipped as God. Not as "a" god, but as God! He claims to sit in the place of God and to have all power and authority over all things. Every pope of Rome has claimed these things for almost two thousand years. The idea that he can forgive the sins of man is foolishness. In Mark 2:7 we read, "Why doth this man thus speak blasphemies? [They were speaking about Jesus] who can forgive sins but God only?"

In Romans 3:23 we find: "For all have sinned, and come short of the glory of God." Did that verse say all have sinned except the pope? No, indeed. It says, "all have sinned." I ask you this one simply question, How can a sinner forgive anyone else's sins?

John 10:33 states that the very act of any man claiming to be equal with God or being able to forgive sin is blasphemy. It says, "The Jews answered him, saying, For a good work we stone thee not; but for blasphemy; and because that thou, being a man, makest thyself God." Get your Bible out, and read this for yourself. Read also Deuteronomy 4:35 and 1 Samuel 2:2.

It is, however, true that there have been many men who have proclaimed themselves as a god, but they neither claimed nor attempted to usurp the status of the one and only true God who created the heavens and the earth. Nor have any of these others (by their own power) changed God's laws; however, by the Catholic Church's own admission, they say they in fact did change the Ten Commandments.

And, instead of proclaiming God's truths, they taught false doctrines and forced the people to accept them while suppressing Bible truths for 1260 years—during which time, history tells us that upwards of one hundred million people were killed simply because they refused to bow down and obey the dictates of those men who claimed to sit in the place of God on earth. This is exactly what God's Word predicted the antichrist would do in Daniel 7:25, which states, in part, "and think to change times and laws," until he was brought down from his lofty perch in AD 1798 by Napoleon's General Berthier.

It was also predicted that his deadly wound would be healed. We find this in Revelation 13:12 where we read: "And he exerciseth all the power of the first beast before him, and causeth the earth and them which dwell therein to worship the first beast, whose deadly wound was healed." History tells us that their power was given back to them by Mussolini in 1929. (Look up the Concordant of 1929.) Then, after regaining their power, they spent the first ten years getting themselves and their organization back on track.

You will also see that the act of tampering with God's laws (the Ten Commandments) is one of the main clues given to find the man the Bible refers to in 2 Thessalonians 2:3 as "the man of sin" and "the son of perdition." And no other human being on the face of this earth has ever, nor will ever, match the numbers 666 with the title of his name, as stated in Revelation 13:18, in three different languages. Luke 23:38 states, "And a superscription also was written over him in letters of Greek, and Latin, and Hebrew." (Check also John 19:20.) It is clear that the heads of the Roman Catholic Church system, the popes themselves, match these descriptions.

As everyone knows in any war, the best way to defeat an enemy is to infiltrate their ranks and begin your battle from the inside. And this has been Satan's strategy from the beginning. Then, after the crucifixion, burial, and resurrection of our Lord Jesus Christ and after the apostles themselves had been killed and taken out of the way, Satan accomplished this through the Catholic Church system.

After reading this, one must ask himself one question, "If the pope is the true mediator between God and man, as each of the popes have claimed over these many years and still claim to this day, why did Jesus Christ shed His blood and die on the cross and claim He was the only mediator between God and man?" As it states in John 14:6, 1 Timothy 2:5, and many other places, Jesus is the mediator between God and man. In fact, doesn't the Bible teach that Jesus' main purpose was to die on the cross and only through the shedding of His blood are we saved?

Allow me to relate a few quotes from the article titled "Pope" in the *Prompta Bibliotheca Canonica*, volume VI, pages 438, 442.

1. "Hence the pope is of so great dignity and so exalted that he is not a man, but as it were God, and the vicar of God." If you look the word vicar up in the dictionary, you will find it refers to someone who sits in place of someone else. Show me if you can from the King James Version Bible where either God or Jesus gave any human this authority. I know there are some who will point to Matthew 16:18-19 and claim that this is where their authority comes from. However, a simple reading from the verse before and the verse after show that Jesus was speaking of "truth" as the "rock." Jesus was saying, "upon this rock [truth] I will build my church." That truth being, "Thou art the Christ," the Son of the living God (Mark 8:29). Read these verses for yourself. (Check also Mark 8:28-30 and Luke 9:18.)

2. "The pope is as it were God, on earth sole sovereign of the faithful of Christ, chief of kings, having plenitude of power, to whom has been entrusted by omnipotent God direction not only of the earthly but also of the heavenly kingdom." Has God placed a mortal man over His heavenly kingdom? Where is this found in the Bible?

3. "So that if it were possible that the angels might err in the faith, or might think contrary to the faith, they could be judged and excommunicated by the pope." Does God allow a mortal man to judge even the angels of heaven? Please, I beg you to show me this from the Bible. Only then will I believe it. Read 1 Kings 8:46 and 2 Chronicles 6:36, which states in part, "for there is no man which sinneth not." Then in 1 John 1:8 we read, "If we say that we have no sin, we deceive ourselves, and the truth is not in us."

4. "The pope can modify divine law [the Ten Commandments], since his power is not of man but of God." The only reference given in the Bible as to man attempting to change God's law is found in Daniel 7:7-8, 20-24— "the little horn"—in 2 Thessalonians 2:3— "the man of sin"— and in Revelation 17:12-13—"the beast." And, if you will go to the library and check out a copy of either *The Convert's Catechism of Catholic Doctrine* or any Catholic Catechism book, you can read these things for yourself. The Catholic Church admits the change of worshipping on Sunday, the first day of the week, instead of Saturday, the seventh day of the week as we are instructed by God Himself. This was not only her act but is a "mark" of her ecclesiastical authority in all religious things. Only through the knowledge of God's Holy Word can these erroneous claims be proven wrong.

At approximately the year AD 62-64, a few of the Christian communities were attempting to incorporate a few of the Old Testament ceremonial laws into the New Testament church. For instance, in Romans 2 we find Paul instructing the Gentile converts that it was wrong for them to hold to the Jewish teaching of every male believer having to be circumcised. While, on the other hand there were other Christian communities who were trying to distance themselves from the Jews, because they also were being persecuted just as the Jews were. So, a few of the leaders of these communities thought that by worshipping on Sunday, as the pagans did, instead of Saturday, or the Sabbath Day as the Jews did and God had commanded, they would escape the persecution. After all, they figured a little compromise with the rest of the world would not hurt.

We find that Paul once again came boldly among them to straighten out this matter. We read his response to this problem in Hebrews 4:1-11. Because it is such a long piece, I will only hit the high points, but I recommend that you get out your Bible and read the whole section. Here are verses 4, 8, 10, and 11. "For he speaks in a certain place of the seventh day on this wise, And God did rest the seventh day from all his works [See Genesis 2:2-3]. For if Jesus had given them rest, then would he not afterward have spoken of another day? For he that is entered into his rest, he also hath ceased from his own works, as God did from his. Let us labour therefore to enter into that rest [speaking of the seventh day], lest any man fall after the same example of unbelief."

Once again, I ask you, could God's Word have made this matter any clearer? Satan was already at work trying to distort Jesus' words and work. Read Hebrews 13:8, which states, "Jesus Christ the same yesterday, and to day, and for ever." God never changes nor does His divine laws, the Ten Commandments.

As you will see for yourselves while reading the article "Vatican Thinking Evolves," the pope is now saying that we may have evolved from some lower life form over millions of years, which simply means that God actually created nothing; therefore, the act of Jesus dying on the cross was of no consequence to the human race at all. Furthermore, Satan is only a figment of our imagination which we made up over the years in order to have someone and or something to blame our sinful ways on. But then, if it is all in our imagination, there can be no actual sin. Which brings us to the conclusion: if we believe these lies, we would probably do just as well if we threw our Bibles away. After all, it would be foolish to believe anything that is written on its pages. If we follow this train of thought and believe these lies, sin isn't sin as we perceive it and we have no true measure by which to judge sin. Therefore, there truly is no right or wrong.

You see, my friend, after reading this information and checking its authenticity for yourself, there is but one question left for you to answer, which is the same question Elijah asked the people of Israel on Mount Carmel, and it will be the question each of us must answer in the very near future. "And Elijah came unto all the people, and said, How long halt ye between two opinions? If the LORD be God, follow him: but if Baal [or, in our case, the pope and his priest and many of today's preachers and Bible teachers], then follow him. And the people answered him not a word" (1 Kings 18:21).

As you know, these were God's chosen people. But when Elijah asked them to choose, they did not know what to do. They had been taught so many different things concerning God and His Holy Word that their thinking was confused. The same is true today. I say this because in 1 Kings 18:17-18 we find the following text: "And it came to pass, when Ahab saw Elijah, that Ahab said unto him, Art thou he that troubleth Israel? And he answered, I have not troubled Israel; but thou, and thy father's house, in that ye have forsaken the commandments of the LORD, and thou hast followed Baalim." This one single issue—following and obeying God's Ten Commandments—has always been, and will be just before Jesus' return, a point of contention between God and His people from the beginning.

This brings us back to what I said before: the people of Israel had been taught so many different things or traditions concerning God and how to truly worship Him that they, as we are today, became so spiritually blinded and confused that they could not distinguish truth from error. On one hand, the pope claims he sits in the place of God on earth and no one comes to the Father but through him; while on the other hand, Jesus states in John 14:6, "I am the way, the truth, and the life: no man cometh unto the Father, but by me."

I always wondered what it meant in Revelation 13:8 when it said, "And all that dwell upon the earth shall worship him, whose names are not written in the book of life of the Lamb slain from the foundation of the world." That is, I wondered about it until I studied God's Word and realized who the beast and what the mark of the beast really was.

"Of course the Catholic Church claims that the change was her act. And the act is a 'mark' of her ecclesiastical authority in religious things," said H.F. Thomas, Chancellor of Cardinal Gibbons.

"Had she not such power, she could not have substituted the observance of Sunday, the first day of the week, for Saturday, the seventh day, a change for which there is no Scriptural authority" (*A Doctrinal Catechism*, p. 174). Now, I ask you, why would the Catholic Church claim to have made these changes if it was not true?

These quotes that I have presented to you prove without a doubt that those who claim we should worship on Sunday, the first day of the week, instead of Saturday, the seventh day of the week, because Jesus rose from the grave on Sunday morning have been and are even now teaching false doctrines. By the Christian world accepting these teachings without question, they are slowly but surely being made ready to accept the mark of the beast.

You see, my friend, the ancient pagan's (Babylonian's) high holy day was Sun Day because they worshipped the sun god Tammuz of which God warned His people not to do. Judges 2:11 states, "And the children of Israel did evil in the sight of the LORD, and served Baalim." Furthermore, Ezekiel 8:14 says, "Then he brought me to the door of the gate of the LORD's house which was toward the north; and, behold, there sat women weeping for Tammuz." (Read also Ezekiel 8:9-18.)

You hold in your hand positive proof of not only who the beast is but also what its mark is. So, who will you believe? Will you believe and follow God our Creator or sinful men, the pope who claims his traditions should be held above God's Holy Word? Remember, the pope even claims that if an angel should sin he can reach into heaven and excommunicate that angel. All the priests and false preachers who go along with whatever the pope says are those who call the information in this book a very radical way of thinking. But then, wasn't the teachings of our Lord Jesus Christ thought of as very radical teachings to the people of His day? And although many have tried, no one has been able to disprove these facts nor any of the following facts that I am about to show you.

By ignoring the historical facts that tie themselves together with these Bible prophecies and articles, people are refusing to accept the simplicity of God's Word which is the only thing that will save them from the second death spoken of in Revelation 21:8: "But the fearful, and unbelieving, and the abominable, and murderers, and whoremongers, and sorcerers, and idolaters, and all liars, shall have their part in the lake which burneth with fire and brimstone: which is the second death."

A BAFFLING MYSTERY

Following is a mystery that has both baffled and confused God's people for almost 2000 long years. "And he shall speak great words against the most High, and shall wear out the saints of the most High, and think to change times and laws: and they shall be given into his hand until a time and times and the dividing of time [1260 days]" (Daniel 7:25). Read also Daniel 12:7; Revelation 11:2-3, 12:6, 12:14, 13:5. Then, in Numbers 14:34 and Ezekiel 4:6, we were instructed to change the 1260 prophetic days into years. By applying these instructions to this 1260 day prophecy, we come up with 1260 years instead of 1260 days. What difference does this make many have asked?

You be the judge. History tells us that in the year AD 330 the Emperor Constantine moved his palace to Constantinople, which was located in the eastern half of what was then the Roman Empire. He referred to Constantinople as his "new Rome." He crowned Pope Silvester I with a triple crown and pronounced him Bishop of Rome and gave him the title of Vicarius Filii Dei or Vicar of the Son of God.

From that very day, the power and authority of the papacy grew and grew until in the year AD 538 they had more power and authority than even the kings. In fact, the popes had gained so much power that they could actually dethrone kings. And each in their turn ruled the world until AD 1798—a total of 1260 years—just as God's prophets predicted they would.

To provide one example of their power, in the eleventh century, Pope Gregory VIII proclaimed the perfection of the Roman Catholic Church. He sent forth a proclamation that declared the following: "The Roman Catholic Church had never, nor can ever err, in any of her decisions."

Furthermore, it is left to the prerogative of the pope to either enthrone or dethrone kings and/or emperors. Also, no one has the power to reverse any sentence or decision made by the pope, but the pope can reverse any decision made by anyone else because both the church and the popes are infallible.

In January 1077 a conflict arose between Pope Gregory and the German King Henry IV over who should yield to whom. For not yielding to the pope's authority, Henry IV was both excommunicated and dethroned. All his household and generals were encouraged by the pope to rebel against this monarch. So terrified and fearful of his own life King Henry felt it necessary to capitulate and surrender to the pope's authority. With his wife and one servant, Henry set out across the Alps in the middle of winter to humble himself before Pope Gregory. Upon arriving he was ushered alone into the courtyard and was made to wait. After three days without food, in the freezing cold, continually making confession of his wrong doings, the Pope finally granted King Henry a pardon.

Their status and power was secure until the year 1798 when the self-proclaimed Emperor Napoleon sent General

Berthier to Rome with orders to take the pope into custody—he died in exile. This event fulfilled two prophecies at one time. The first is found in Revelation 13:10, "He that leadeth into captivity shall go into captivity: he that killeth with the sword must be killed with the sword. Here is the patience and the faith of the saints." The second is found in the first half of verse 3 of that same chapter: "And I saw one of his heads as it were wounded to death."

But in the second half of Revelation 13:3, we find the prophecy which relates to what I spoke of a few pages back when Mussolini executed what is known as "The Concordat of 1929," which restored to the papacy all their properties and powers. This is what is meant by "his deadly wound was healed."

At this point it is very important for us to remember that Daniel 2 and 7 are parallel chapters. In other words, Nebuchadnezzar's dream has the same meanings as the four beasts of Daniel's vision. Each section of the statue represents the same four nations as the four beasts:

1. Babylon - the head of gold or the lion with eagles wings

2. Medo-Persia - the arms folded across the silver breast or the bear with the three ribs in its mouth

3. Greece - the belly and thighs of brass or the leopard with wings and four heads

4. Rome - the two legs of iron and feet of part iron and part clay or the beast that was dreadful and terrible and strong and had great iron teeth and had ten horns and was diverse (different) from all the beasts that were before it

"I [Daniel] considered the horns, and, behold, there came up among them [the first ten horns] another little horn, before whom there were three of the first horns plucked up by the roots: and, behold, in this horn were eyes like the eyes of man, and a mouth speaking great things" (Daniel 7:8).

I would now draw your attention to the two legs of the statue. As you remember, after Constantinople was finished, Emperor Constantine moved the seat of his government there— a move that divided the Roman territories into east and west. This division is what the two legs of the statue represent—a division that has lasted throughout history to our day, just as the Bible predicted it would in Daniel 2:43.

In Daniel 7:15-16 we are told that Daniel was very troubled. As he prayed and asked for guidance, he was given the answers: "These great beasts, which are four, are four kings, which shall arise out of the earth" (verse 17). "The fourth beast shall be the fourth kingdom upon earth, which shall be diverse from all kingdoms, and shall devour the whole earth, and shall tread it down, and break it into pieces. And the ten horns out of this kingdom are ten kings that shall arise: and another shall rise after them; and he shall be diverse [different] from the first, and he shall subdue three kings. And he shall speak great words against the most High, and shall wear out the saints of the most High, and think to change times and laws: and they [the saints] shall be given into his hand until a time and times and the dividing of time" (verses 23-25)—or three and a half years, which we translate into 1260 days, which according to Numbers 14:34 and Ezekiel 4:6 is converted into 1260 years.

Did you catch what it said concerning the eleventh horn? It shall arise *after* the other ten are already in place, and it would be a diverse or different kind of kingdom than the first ten.

Looking back through history we find that the ten nations that came out of the Old Romam Empire were the Franks, the Suevi, the Anglo Saxons, the Ostrogoths, the

Vandals, the Visigoths, the Heruli, the Lombards, the Burgundians, and the Alamanni. But prophecy tells us that three of these ten nations were to be plucked up (overthrown) by the roots.

History indicates that three nations were overthrown: the Heruli in AD 493, the Vandals in AD 534, and the Ostrogoths in AD 538. Once the last of the three nations fell, Pope Vigilius, the 59th pope who reigned from AD 537-555, referred back to two proclamations (royal edicts), which were claimed to have been given to the papacy by Emperor Justinian in AD 533. One recognized the pope's ecclesiastical supremacy as "head of all the holy churches" in both the east and west while the other legally proclaimed and confirmed the pope as "the bishop of Rome" and "head of all the holy priests of God." As you will see, by doing this Satan, working through Emperor Justintian, fulfilled the prophecy of Revelation 13:2: "and the dragon gave him his power, and his seat, and great authority."

In Revelation 13:1-2 we find another beast: "And I stood upon the sand of the sea, and saw a beast rise up out of the sea, having seven heads and ten horns, and upon his horns ten crowns, and upon his heads the name of blasphemy. And the beast which I saw was like unto a leopard, and his feet were as the feet of a bear, and his mouth as the mouth of a lion: and the dragon gave him his power, and his seat, and great authority."

Speaking of this dragon, have you ever wondered just who or what this "dragon" represents? I realize there are a lot of theories, but if you will simply turn to Revelation 12:9, you will no longer have any doubt. We read: "And the great dragon was cast out, that old serpent, called the Devil, and Satan, which deceiveth the whole world: he was cast out into the earth, and his angels were cast out with him."

So, by this we can conclude that the dragon, that old serpent the devil or Satan, whatever you wish to call him, has and will continue to work through this apostate religious church system until the second coming of our Lord Jesus Christ, at which time Satan shall be chained (figuratively speaking because of circumstances) for a thousand years.

Now, let's look at Revelation 17 where you will find yet another beast. And as you will see, this new beast and the beast of Revelation 13 are also connected with one another just as the statue and beast of Daniel 2 and 7 are connected to these two as is the next beast we will study in a moment. The thing to remember is that each of these beasts represent a different kingdom, nation, or age in the timeline of history.

The same is also true of the seven churches, the seven trumpets, the seven seals, the seven lamp stands, the seven last plagues, etc. (These are covered in another book that is now in progress.)

BABYLON THE GREAT, THE MOTHER OF HARLOTS

When referring to His true followers (the true church), Jesus called them "His bride," true and holy. So, common sense tells us that a "harlot" would be just the opposite—impure and unholy—but it could be a church none the less. As before, God's Holy Word will explain exactly what these things mean.

Beginning in Revelation 17:1-7, we read: "And there came one of the seven angels which had the seven vials, and talked with me, saying unto me, Come hither; I will shew unto thee the judgment of the great whore that sitteth upon many waters: With whom the kings of the earth have committed fornication, and the inhabitants of the earth have been made drunk with the wine of her fornication. So he carried me away in the spirit into the wilderness: and I saw a woman sit upon a scarlet coloured beast, full of names of blasphemy, having seven heads and ten horns.

"And the woman was arrayed in purple and scarlet colour, and decked with gold and precious stones and pearls, having a golden cup in her hand full of abominations and filthiness of her fornication: And upon her forehead was a name written, MYSTERY, BABYLON THE GREAT, THE MOTHER OF HARLOTS AND ABOMINATIONS OF THE EARTH.

"And I saw the woman drunken with the blood of the saints, and with the blood of the martyrs of Jesus: and when I saw her, I wondered with great admiration. And the angel said unto me, Wherefore didst thou marvel? I will tell thee the mystery of the woman, and of the beast that carrieth her, which hath the seven heads and ten horns."

Now, let's look at verse 9 where we find the answers to this puzzle: "And here is the mind which hath wisdom. The seven heads are seven mountains, on which the woman sitteth."

A quick comment concerning these seven mountains: you can search all the world history books from the beginning of time, and you will find that in the whole world there have only been two cities that are said to sit on, or within, seven mountains. Today, there is only one. These two locations are Lisbon, Portugal, and Rome, Italy. The reason there is only one today is because on November 1, 1780, the largest earthquake ever recorded in history hit Lisbon. The tremors were felt over four million square miles. This earthquake was followed by histories largest tidal wave, which not only leveled Lisbon, but also leveled the surrounding hills for up to fifty square miles from the center of town. This leaves only the seven hills of Rome.

As to the sea or waters mentioned in Revelation 17:1 and other places, look at verse 15: "And he saith unto me, The waters which thou sawest, where the whore sitteth, are peoples, and multitudes, and nations, and tongues."

Therefore, the location can only be on the continent of Europe, and the timeframe can only be from AD 538 through

AD 1798, which is exactly 1260 years—the same time beginning with the ten nation split of the Old Roman Empire of which three fell or in other words were overthrown. Look at it for yourself.

This beast parallels the "little horn" mentioned in Daniel 7. As you can see, they both have similar points of interest. They not only look somewhat alike, but they also have the following characteristics:

- "And there was given unto him a mouth speaking great things and blasphemies" (Revelation 13:5).

- "And power was given unto him to continue forty and two months [a time, times, and a half a time]" (Revelation 13:5)

- "And it was given unto him to make war with the saints, and overcome them" (Revelation 13:7).

This brings us to one of the most important clues of this whole study, which is found in Revelation 13:17-18: "And that no man might buy or sell, save he that had the mark, or the name of the beast, or the number of his name. Here is wisdom. Let him that hath understanding count the number of the beast: for it is the number of a man; and his number is Six hundred threescore and six [666]." By changing the letters of the pope's title, which is Vicarius Filii Dei, into numbers, this is what you come up with in three different languages:

LATIN

V = 5	F = 0	D = 500
I = 1	I = 1	E = 0
C = 100	L = 50	I = 1
A = 0	I = 1	501
R = 0	I = 1	112
I = 1	53	+53
U = 5		666
S = 0		
112		

Some have asked, "Is this phrase found on the pope's mitre (triple-crown) today?" The answer is NO. Back in the middle of the seventeenth century, the Catholic Church was embarrassed by what a man figured out by following the instructions in Revelation 13:17-18 and changing the letters into numbers, so the phrase was removed. That phrase was

GREEK (Latin man or Church)	HEBRON - ROMIITH (Roman - Kingdom)
A = 30	= 200
A = 1	= 6
T = 300	= 40
E = 5	= 10
I = 10	= 10
N = 50	= 400
O = 70	666
Z = 200	
666	

"Vicarius Filii Dei," which simply means "Vicar of the Son of God." However, the Roman Catholic Church continues to use this phrase in their ceremonies when a new pope is ordained. Therefore, "Vicarius Filii Dei" (Vicar of the Son of God), is still the pope's official title.

Why three different languages you may ask? Because in John 19:20 we read, "This title then read many of the Jews: for the place where Jesus was crucified was nigh to the city: and it was written in Hebrew, Greek, and Latin." (See also verse 19.)

But remember, this (as with all the other clues) in and of itself proves nothing. For us to track down the rest of the information, we need to remember one of the other main prophecies, which is given to locate this so called "man of sin." Go back to Daniel 7:25, which reads: "he shall . . . think to change times and laws."

Although many will argue with this, this statement is referring to God's laws—the Ten Commandments. And, the Roman Catholic Church claims that by their power they changed the Ten Commandments.

To review this for yourself simply go to the nearest library and check out *The Convert's Catechism of Catholic Doctrine* where you will find the following question and answer discussion concerning their changed set of God's laws.

Q. "What is the Third Commandment?"

A. "The Third Commandment is: Remember that thou keep holy the Sabbath day."

According to Scripture, if you will check Exodus 20, you will find it is the fourth commandment that refers to keeping the Sabbath day holy. But, as you can see, the Catholic Church has omitted the third commandment which refers to making and worshipping graven images, since the church promotes worshipping the virgin Mary or statues of dead saints.

I realize I have upset a lot of people, but I am telling you these things out of my love for you. God would not have you ignorant of these facts. Right now, you still have the freedom to choose. Not too long into the future the time is soon coming when that choice will be made for you by force. In the very near future, Jesus will step from the judgment hall in heaven and proclaim, "He that is unjust, let him be unjust still: and he which is filthy, let him be filthy still: and he that is righteous, let him be righteous still: and he that is holy, let him be holy still" (Revelation 22:11). Then it will be too late.

By comparing these two sets of commandments (which follow), you can see right away that they have not only removed the third commandment but have also moved the fourth commandment up to take its place. Furthermore, they divided the tenth commandment into two parts in order to once again have ten commandments.

As you can clearly see, all the instructions that explain what a graven image is, what day God's true Sabbath is on, and who created the heavens and the earth have been stripped away. This leaves it to "their" discretion to explain these things to us, which in itself is the biggest mistake any person could ever make. When you leave it up to any man or woman to explain God's Word to you, you have left yourself open for trouble. I have always believed that when it concerns God's Word always check everything out for yourself.

Following are the two sets of the Ten Commandments I spoke of before:

The Law of God
According to Exodus 20:3-17
1. "Thou shalt have no gods before me."
2. "Thou shalt not make unto thee any graven image, or any likeness of anything that is in heaven above, or that is in the earth beneath, or that is in the water under the earth. Thou shalt not bow down thyself to them, nor serve them, for I the Lord thy God am a jealous God, visiting the iniquity of the fathers upon the children unto the third and fourth generation of them that hate me; and showing mercy unto thousands of them that love me, and keep my commandments."
3. "Thou shalt not take the name of the Lord thy God in vain; for the Lord will not hold him guiltless that taketh His name in vain."
4. "Remember the Sabbath day, to keep it holy. Six days shalt thou labor, and do all thy work; but the seventh day is the Sabbath of the Lord thy God. In it thou shalt not do any work, thou, nor thy son, nor thy daughter, thy manservant, not thy maidservant, not thy cattle, nor thy stranger that is within thy gates. For in six days the Lord made heaven and earth, the sea, and all that in them is, and rested the seventh day: Wherefore the Lord blessed the Sabbath day, and hallowed it."
5. "Honor thy father and thy mother, that thy days may be long upon the land which the Lord thy God giveth thee."
6. "Thou shalt not kill."
7. Thou shalt not commit adultery."
8. "Thou shalt not steal."
9. "Thou shalt not bear false witness against thy neighbor."
10. "Thou shalt not covet thy neighbor's house; thou shalt not covet thy neighbor's wife, nor his manservant, nor his maidservant nor his ox, nor his ass, nor anything that is thy neighbor's."

The Law of God
as Changed by the Catholic Church
These commandments are as listed in the General Catholic Catechism.
1. "I am the Lord thy God. Thou shalt not have strange gods before Me." (The second commandment has been omitted so the church's second commandment is God's third.)
2. "Thou shalt not take the name of the Lord thy God in vain."
3. "Remember that thou keep holy the Sabbath day." (The third commandment has been radically altered to fit their belief system.)
4. "Honor thy father and thy mother."
5. "Thou shalt not kill."
6. "Thou shalt not commit adultery."
7. "Thou shalt not steal."
8. "Thou shalt not bear false witness against thy neighbor."
9. "Thou shalt not covet thy neighbor's wife." (The ninth commandment is actually the first part of God's tenth commandment.)
10. "Thou shalt not covet thy neighbor's goods." (This is the second part of God's tenth commandment.)

Now, with these facts before us, let's continue with the question and answer discussion we were referencing from The Convert's Catechism of Catholic Doctrine.

Q. "Which is the Sabbath day?"

A. "Saturday is the Sabbath day."

Q. "Why do we observe Sunday instead of Saturday?"

A. "We observe Sunday instead of Saturday because the Catholic Church transferred the Solemnity from Saturday to Sunday."

Q. "Why did the Catholic Church substitute Sunday for Saturday?"

A. "The Church substituted Sunday for Saturday, because Christ rose from the dead on a Sunday, and the Holy Ghost descended upon the Apostles on Sunday."

Q. "By what authority did the Church substitute Sunday for Saturday?"

A. "The Church substituted Sunday for Saturday by the plenitude of that divine power which Jesus Christ bestowed upon her."

Q. "What does the Third Commandment command?"

A. "The Third Commandment commands us to sanctify Sunday as the Lord's Day."

Did this last answer seem contrary to the discussion? Well, it is not if read right. You see, my friend, the key word is *us*, which refers only to Catholics and does not include Protestants—or "separated brethren" as we Protestants are referred to by the Catholic hierarchies. And, I want to also show you before we get too far ahead that Protestants have their own generic set of the Ten Commandments. In fact, it is making its way around the United States as I write this. Although they are, for the most part, the same Ten Commandments listed in Exodus 20, this set also has no explanation of what day of the week the Sabbath falls on or what constitutes an idol. Let me show you what I mean:

1. "Thou shalt have no other gods before Me."
2. "Thou shalt not make unto thee any graven image."
3. "Thou shalt not take the name of the Lord thy God in vain."
4. "Remember the Sabbath day, to keep it holy."
5. "Honor thy father and mother."
6. "Thou shalt not kill."
7. "Thou shalt not commit adultery."
8. "Thou shalt not steal."
9. "Thou shalt not bear false witness against thy neighbor."
10. "Thou shalt not covet thy neighbor's wife, or goods."

There are many preachers out there who tell their congregation that as long as they follow these ten simple rules (at least as close as they can of course) and say their prayers every night then they have done all that God has asked them to do.

Well, my friends, I'm not sure that is right. The reason I say this is because almost 95 percent of all professed Christians do not know that they are not even worshiping God on His day—the Sabbath Day—as He instructed us to do. I realize that there are those out there who claim the days of the week have been changed so many times through the years that it makes no difference what day we worship God on. However, I believe that this is a lie. Although there has been one change made in our calendar (I will explain that a little later), the cycle of the days were never changed. Even if this were true, consider the following points.

In the Old Testament, there are 126 references to the Sabbath. All these texts are harmonious in voicing the will of God commanding the seventh day to be kept because God Himself first kept it, thereby making it obligatory on all who claim to be His children as a perpetual covenant. I cannot imagine anyone questioning the identity of the Sabbath day as being Saturday, seeing that the people of Israel have been observing and keeping it from the giving of the law in 2514 BC and are still keeping it to this very day, some 4,500 years.

After examining the New Testament, from cover to cover, you will find the Sabbath is referred to 61 times. You will also find that Jesus invariably selected the Sabbath day to teach in the synagogues and also work miracles. The four Gospels alone refer to the Sabbath 51 times.

Meanwhile, from Genesis to Revelation, you will find the first day is mentioned 43 times, with most of these referring to either the first day of the month or the first day of the feast (see Matthew 26:17). Matthew 28:1, Mark 16:1-2, Luke 24:1, and John 20:1 document the fact that after the Sabbath had passed, some came to the tomb to anoint Jesus' body early in the morning on the first day of the week. Mark 16:9 also reports that Jesus rose early the first day of the week and appeared first to Mary Magdalene. Each writer was sure to add "after the Sabbath had passed."

One must ask themselves, "If this is true, and the true Sabbath is Saturday instead of Sunday, why isn't this being taught by all the Protestant preachers? Why are they claiming either Sunday is the new Sabbath or that it does not really matter which day we worship on?" Let's consider this next bit of information.

There are some who point to John 20:1-9 and declare these verses prove that we are to keep Sunday holy simply because Jesus rose from the tomb and appeared to the disciples on Sunday, the first day of the week.

I think this next tidbit of information is very important to our study. We find what we are looking for in John 20:19: "Then the same day at evening, being the first day of the week, when the doors were shut where the disciples were assembled for fear of the Jews, came Jesus and stood in the midst, and saith unto them, Peace be unto you."

I believe that the only thing this verse proves is that Jesus kept the fourth commandment by resting in the tomb on the Sabbath day, and then, on Sunday, he went to give comfort to his frightened disciples who were cowering in an out-of-the-way apartment in fear of the Roman soldiers and the Jewish religious leaders who may find them.

Then, in Acts 20:7 we read that on the evening of the first day of the week when the disciples came together to break bread Paul preached until midnight. This breaking of bread was only an evening meal; it had nothing to do with Sunday being a holy day. The reason I say this is because if you look at verse 11 you will see that they broke bread again that same night and continued talking until almost sunrise because Paul was on his way to Jerusalem and would not be seeing them for awhile.

Now, I ask you, how can this verse be considered anything more than what we today call a Bible study to encourage one another? Of course, they did not have Bibles to study from; Paul was relating things the Master had taught and shown him. But some people claim that these meetings prove that these people were worshipping on Sunday.

Some of today's preachers even point to 1 Corinthians 16:1-2 and claim that this is one of the verses that proves without a doubt that Sunday is the Sabbath day. It states: "Now concerning the collection for the saints, as I have given order to the churches of Galatia, even so do ye. Upon the first day of the week let every one of you lay by him in store, as God hath prospered him, that there be no gathering when I come."

As you can see, this verse is referring to the collection of offerings. How does this prove the Sabbath was changed from Saturday to Sunday? These verses I have shown you fit in the same category as Acts 11:29 and 24:17; each is speaking of offerings to help pay the church bills and help families in need.

Many of today's Protestant preachers and Bible teachers refer to Sunday, the first day of the week, either as the Lord's day or as the Christian Sabbath, claiming it was changed because our Lord rose from the tomb on Sunday. Furthermore, they refer to Easter Sunday as one of the most holy Sundays of all. But, as we have found in our study booklet *The Origin of Easter* this day is one of the most pagan days, which started thousands of years ago in Babylon.

There are also many preachers and Bible teachers who use Romans 14:5-6 to prove that it does not matter what day we worship on, thus justifying Sunday observance over Saturday observance.

Now, while I agree that we can go to church and study God's Word on any day of the week, I still contend that nowhere in the Holy Bible can you or anyone else find a single verse that supports this change of the Sabbath day from the seventh day to the first day of the week. Instead, as I have said before, I find quite the opposite. Let's take a look at Romans 14:5-6 and find out for ourselves exactly what these two verses are telling us.

"One man esteemeth one day above another: another esteemeth every day alike. Let every man be fully persuaded in his own mind. He that regardeth the day [referring to the Sabbath day], regardeth it unto the Lord; and he that regardeth not the day, to the Lord he doth not regard it. He that eateth, eateth to the Lord, for he giveth God thanks [he prays before eating], and he that eateth not, to the Lord he eateth not, and giveth God thanks."

Even today there are those who worship on different days. For some, their holy day is Thursday, while others it is Friday, still others it is Saturday or Sunday. It was no different then. Just as some today won't eat certain animals because they suppose them to be unholy or sacred. If you will look at the last part of Romans 14:5, you will find this advice: "Let every man be fully persuaded in his own mind." This simply means that each of us has a choice.

Also, read 1 Timothy 4:1-5. Will we choose to worship God on His terms or do we expect God to meet us on our terms? We should never condemn others for the choices they have made or will make; however, as a Christian it is my obligation to inform others of what God's Holy Word really says on these matters. Of course, it is up to you to chose who you will follow. Will you observe and follow His laws as He has laid before you in Holy Scripture or not?

In Romans 13:9, we find the following: "For this, Thou shalt not commit adultery, Thou shalt not kill, Thou shalt not steal, Thou shalt not bear false witness, Thou shalt not covet; and if there be any other commandment, it is briefly comprehended in this saying, namely, Thou shalt love thy neighbor as thyself." Paul himself is affirming that the Ten Commandments are in fact still in affect. By this, we know that all of the Ten Commandments were still observed. There was not any reason for these early Christians to be reminded of the Sabbath day commandment specifically when the statement "and if there be any other commandment, it is briefly comprehended in this saying" was used. If you look back at Romans 12:2, you will find that Paul had just told them, "And be not conformed to this world: but be ye transformed by the renewing of your mind, that ye may prove what is that good, and acceptable, and perfect, will of God."

It is like my grandmother used to say, "If the rest of the world went and jumped off a cliff, does that mean you would too?" You see, my friend, the question is "Are you willing to go against the teachings of those false religious leaders (as the disciples did in their day) and observe all ten of God's commandments? Or will you go along with the rest of the world and hope for the best?"

I direct your attention to Hebrews 4:8 where we read, "For if Jesus had given them rest, then would he not afterward have spoken of another day." Of all the preachers and/or teachers whom I have heard try to prove that Sunday is the Sabbath day, I have never heard anyone quote from this chapter. And I must ask, "Could it be because these few words would prove their whole theory wrong? Why does almost the whole Christian world go along with this lie?"

Let me show you one last example before moving on to the next topic. Many, when referring to the Sabbath, call it "the Lord's day" and direct your attention to Revelation 1:10, claiming this verse refers to Sunday. But I ask you, "Does the Lord God have a certain day of the week that He values more than any of the other six days?" The answer is yes. God has always had a certain day that He values above all other days. And from the beginning of Holy Scripture even unto the end, this "day" is spoken of. Let's take a closer look at Revelation 1:10: "I was in the Spirit on the Lord's day, and heard behind me a great voice, as a trumpet." Now remember, John lived in a time when it was a natural thing to refer to the Sabbath day as the Lord's day because everyone knew which "day" he spoke of. Allow me to show you a few places where this day is mentioned in Scripture.

Beginning in Genesis 2:2-3 we read, "And on the seventh day God ended his work which he had made; and he rested on the seventh day from all his work which he had made. And God blessed the seventh day, and sanctified it: because that in it he had rested from all his work which God created and made."

Turn now to Exodus 20:8-11: "Remember the sabbath day, to keep it holy. Six days shalt thou labour, and do all thy work: But the seventh day is the sabbath of the Lord thy God: in it thou shalt not do any work, thou, nor thy son, nor thy daughter, thy manservant, nor thy maidservant, nor thy cattle, nor thy stranger that is within thy gates: For in six days the LORD made heaven and earth, the sea, and all that in them is, and rested the seventh day: wherefore the LORD blessed the sabbath day, and hallowed it."

In fact, this day was considered such a "holy day" to God that we read in Exodus 35:2, "Six days shall work be done, but on the seventh day there shall be to you an holy day, a sabbath of rest to the LORD: whosoever doeth work therein shall be put to death." Also, read Leviticus 23:3. But for this study, let's skip over to Deuteronomy 5 where from verses 6-21 the Ten Commandments are repeated. We find in verse 12, "Keep the sabbath day to sanctify it, as the LORD thy God hath commanded thee."

Now, let's turn to Deuteronomy 11 and take a look at verses 26-28: "Behold, I set before you this day a blessing and a curse; a blessing, if ye obey the commandments of the

LORD your God, which I command you this day: And a curse, if ye will not obey the commandments of the LORD your God, but turn aside out of the way which I command you this day, to go after other gods, which ye have not known."

Also, read Deuteronomy 26:16-19. Allow me to show you verses 17-18: "Thou hast avouched [declared] the LORD this day to be thy God, and to walk in his ways, and to keep his statutes, and his commandments, and his judgments, and to hearken unto his voice: And the LORD hath avouched thee this day to be his peculiar people, as he hath promised thee, and that thou shouldest keep all his commandments."

I know many are saying right now that God is speaking to the Jews here (and that in a sense is true, at least for that time in history), but if you have read study booklet #1, then you know that the Jews (as a nation) were cut out of God's promises because of their unbelief and the gentiles (individual Christians believing Jesus Christ was and is the Son of God veiled in human flesh and is our only Lord and Savior) were grafted in, in their place. Read Deuteronomy 27:1, 28:1-2; Romans 11:17-21; and Hebrews 4:1-11 for clarification.

From Exodus 31:12-18, I will quote verses 16-17: "Wherefore the children of Israel [Jacob] shall keep the sabbath, to observe the sabbath throughout their generations, for a perpetual covenant. It is a sign between me and the children of Israel [Jacob] for ever: for in six days the LORD made heaven and earth, and on the seventh day he rested, and was refreshed."

Again, if you have read study #1, then you know that by accepting Jesus Christ as your Lord and Savior you are spiritually considered a descendant of "Jacob," whose name was changed by God to "Israel." This is why I tell everyone I speak with that many times when Scripture refers to "Israel" or the "children of Israel" it is referring to the descendants of "Jacob," as in Hosea 12:4. Read Genesis 32:28 for confirmation of this fact.

Leaving the Old Testament and moving to the New Testament, we continue exploring the truth about the Sabbath. We begin in Matthew 12:8: "For the Son of man is Lord even of the sabbath day." Then, in Mark 2:27-28 it says, "And he said unto them, The sabbath was made for man, and not man for the sabbath: Therefore the Son of man is Lord also of the sabbath."

Now, let's look at John 14:15: "If ye love me, keep my commandments." And 1 John 5:2-3 says, "By this we know that we love the children of God, when we love God and keep his commandments. For this is the love of God, that we keep his commandments: and his commandments are not grievous."

In James 2:10 we find the following: "For whosoever shall keep the whole law, and yet offend in one point, he is guilty of all." There can be no doubt that James is speaking of the Ten Commandments once we read verses 11 and 12 of that same chapter: "For he that said, Do not commit adultery, said also, Do not kill. Now if thou commit no adultery, yet if thou kill, thou art become a transgressor of the law. So speak ye, and so do, as they that shall be judged by the law of liberty."

At this point, let me ask one simple question: Why, out of all the Ten Commandments, is there so much disagreement and controversy throughout Christendom concerning the fourth commandment? Just think about it for a moment. Imagine that you own a big corporation. If I can raise a doubt in the minds of a few of the other workers concerning something you have said or done (whether it is true or not), then I have not only taken a little of your authority away but I have also changed the way others look at you. Of course, you are still who you are, but I have brought you down a few notches so to speak. Well, this has been Satan's plan from the beginning. Then, once he had one third of the angels in heaven on his side, he started his rebellion. Let me show you what I mean.

Take the fourth commandment and break it apart. What do we find? In the first eight words we are told to "Remember the sabbath day, to keep it holy." But, as we saw earlier, after the second commandment was taken out (the one dealing with not worshipping graven images or idols) these same eight words formed the whole third commandment. But, if you will look back at the original set of the Ten Commandments, you will read in the last 14 words of the second commandment, "and shewing mercy unto thousands of them that love me, and keep my commandments." This is why the Catholic Church omitted the third commandment. With it in place, they would not have been able to incorporate and dominate all the other heathen religions.

God goes on to explain how the Sabbath is to be remembered. "Six days shalt thou labour, and do all thy work; but the seventh day is the sabbath of the LORD thy God: in it thou shalt not do any work, thou, nor thy son, nor thy daughter, thy manservant, nor thy maidservant, nor thy cattle, nor thy stranger that is within thy gates" (Exodus 20:9-10). All work must stop.

Then God tells us why the Sabbath is to be remembered in this particular way. "For in six days the LORD made heaven and earth, the sea, and all that in them is, and rested the seventh day: wherefore the LORD blessed the seventh day, and hallowed it" (verse 11). As you can see, this last section tells us why we should honor this day, because by us honoring this day, we are in fact honoring God as our Creator.

We find in Psalms 124:8, "Our help is in the name of the LORD, who made heaven and earth." In Acts 4:24 we find, "And when they heard that, they lifted up their voice to God with one accord, and said, Lord, thou art God, which hast made heaven, and earth, and the sea, and all that in them is." See also Acts 14:15, 2 Kings 19:15.

So, with this information I have given you so far, you know who the antichrist is (also referred to as the little horn in Daniel 7:8) and that he ruled and will rule until God takes him out of the way from atop the seven hills of Rome for those 1260 years spoken of in Daniel 7:25, 12:7; Revelation 11:2-3, 12:6, 12:14, and 13:5. We also learned that the beast who received a deadly wound that was healed is really a worldwide religious/secular system and that the mark of the beast is actually the act of worshipping on Sunday, the first day of the week, instead of Saturday, the seventh day of the week.

Now, I know there are some out there who are asking, "How can Sunday even be considered the mark of the beast? Doesn't it say in Revelation 13:16-17 that everyone would receive a mark either in their right hand or their forehead?" Yes, it does say that. Allow me to answer this question here, although it will be repeated later in the book.

You see, my friend, if you think of it either as a day or a thing it cannot be seen as a mark. But when you think of it in symbolic terms (of which all prophecies are made up of) then it can be a mark. Let me explain. Let's read Revelation 13:16-17 and see what it actually says. "And he causeth all, both small and great, rich and poor, free and bond, to receive a mark in their right hand, or in their foreheads: And that no man might buy or sell, save he that had the mark, or the name of the beast, or the number of his name."

Let's break this verse down and see what we find. Take the first portion: "And he causeth all." He can be referring to none other than the antichrist who will once again rule the world during the closing days of earth's history.

Now, take the next portion: "both small and great, rich and poor, free and bond." As you can see, this encompasses all humanity on earth.

The next portion tells us that all humanity will be made to "receive a mark in their right hand, or in their foreheads." If anyone swears to something (whether they personally believe it or not), they swear by raising their right hand and swearing. Am I right? But, if you truly believe in your mind that something is true, then you believe it in your forehead or what is called your invisible third eye. Why, you may ask, would someone swear to something they don't believe? Well, the very next verse answers this question.

The first part reads, "And that no man might buy or sell, save he that had the mark." Now, common sense tells us that when it comes to the point of not being able to buy food or things your family may need most people will swear to anything by saying "I believe what you are saying is true." After all, how many people get on the witness stand in court and swear to something they know to be a lie? Of course, this isn't to say you won't be made to receive some kind of an implanted chip for identification when you go to buy groceries or whatever. The implantation of an identification locator chip is now a common thing for dogs and cats. It is not a stretch of the imagination to think that some sort of locater chip could be implanted in humans as well.

The second part reads "or the name of the beast." These are people who already belong to or are in some way connected with this worldwide religious/secular organization but will consist of both unsuspecting Catholics and Christians in the last days. Therefore, they won't have to swear to anything because they already believe what these people are telling them is true.

Then, the third part states "or the number of his name." This part speaks of the popes who have headed this false religion from its starts in approximately AD 538 until our Lord's return in the clouds of heaven.

And speaking of "the mark," millions don't realize that God also has His own mark or seal which His people (the true believers) will receive. And, only by receiving His mark will they be saved in the final minutes of earth's history. We find this in Revelation 7:2-3, which states, "And I saw another angel ascending from the east, having the seal of the living God: and he cried with a loud voice to the four angels, to whom it was given to hurt the earth and the sea, Saying, Hurt not the earth, neither the sea, nor the trees, till we have sealed the servants of our God in their foreheads."

These people can only be those that honor God by keeping the fourth commandment (which is the seal of God's authority) and truly believe that God is the creator of all things and only through the shed blood of Jesus Christ can they have any hope of salvation.

Remember, we are told in Isaiah 28:9-13 and 29:13-14 that "precept must be upon precept, precept upon precept, line upon line, line upon line; here a little, and there a little" (Isaiah 28:10). So, with this in mind, turn to Ezekiel 9:4-6, where we read, "And the LORD said unto him, Go through the midst of the city, through the midst of Jerusalem, and set a mark upon the foreheads of the men that sigh and that cry for all the abominations that be done in the midst thereof. And to the others he said in mine hearing, Go ye after him through the city, and smite: let not your eye spare, neither have pity: Slay utterly old and young, both maids, and little children, and women: but come not near any man upon whom is the mark; and begin at my sanctuary. Then they began at the ancient men which were before the house."

Do you remember when God was about to bring the children of Israel out of Egypt? He instructed Moses and Aaron to have the people slay lambs and put the blood on the top and both sides of their doorpost so that when the death angel passed through the streets killing all the first-born of Egypt he would pass by the houses with blood on the doorpost, not touching anyone in that house. You will find this in Exodus 12. As you can see, they either followed God's instructions or they died. It will be the same when Jesus comes in the clouds of heaven to receive His elect from the four corners of this earth. There will be no if, ands, or buts—either follow God's instructions or die. Simple as that. It is completely your decision. Do not allow anyone to cheat you out of God's promise.

God will place His seal in their foreheads. You will find references of God's seal in Revelation 7:3, 9:4, 14:1, 20:4, and 22:4.

THE WOMAN AND
THE DRAGON

In Revelation 12 we find a woman and a great red dragon: "And there appeared a great wonder in heaven; a woman clothed with the sun, and the moon under her feet, and upon her head a crown of twelve stars."

There are many preachers who both claim and teach that this woman who is clothed with the sun, has the moon under her feet, and a crown of twelve stars on her head is Mary, the mother of Jesus. But, as you will see, nothing is farther from the truth. This chapter is depicting the age of the New Testament church, stretching from the birth of our Lord Jesus Christ through the dark ages to His second coming.

To begin with, this woman is symbolic of the bride of Christ (the church). She is both pure and holy. In Jeremiah 6:2 we find: "I have likened the daughter of Zion to a comely and delicate woman." We find in 2 Corinthians 11:2, "For I am jealous over you with godly jealousy: for I have espoused you to one husband, that I may present you as a chaste virgin to Christ."

The sun is symbolic of the light of the true gospel. We find in Psalms 27:1: "The LORD is my light and my salvation; whom shall I fear? the LORD is the strength of my life; of whom shall I be afraid?" Also Psalms 84:11 says, "For the LORD is a sun and shield: the LORD will give grace and glory: no good thing will he withhold from them that walk uprightly." While in Psalms 119:105, we read, "Thy word is a lamp unto my feet, and a light unto my path."

In Romans 13:12 we find: "The night is far spent, the day is at hand: let us therefore cast off the works of darkness, and let us put on the armour of light." Then, in 1 John 2:8 we read: "Again, a new commandment I write unto you, which thing is true in him and in you: because the darkness is past, and the true light now shineth." Now turn to 1 Corinthians 13:12, where we read, "For now we see through a glass, darkly; but then face to face: now I know in part; but then shall I know even as also I am known." See also 1 John 3:2 and Isaiah 56:5.

The moon is a representation of the light of the gospel dimming through the erroneous teachings of unscrupulous men who were at work even while the disciples were still alive (see Galatians 1:6-8) and of the apostate church up through those 1260 long years of which I spoke of earlier, while the twelve stars represent the twelve apostles.

I will quickly run through Revelation 12. Verses 2 and 5 refer to the condition of the Jews just before the birth of Jesus. They knew their long awaited Savior was about to come because of the signs they had been given to look for. (Just as we, in our time, are given certain signs to look for which will tell us His second coming is near). Unfortunately, the Jewish holy men had the people so bogged down in traditions that they did not have a chance to get used to one thing before they were confronted with something else. You see, it had been so long since God had spoken to anyone and the holy men had drifted so far away from God's true Word that they were placing their traditions above God's Word.

Even Jesus himself was a big surprise to the common people simply because most believed He would be some great warrior who would come to free them from their Roman oppressors. This was what many of their religious teachers had taught them. When Jesus appeared and taught them to love their enemies instead of hating them and retaliating against them, He spoke contrary to what the Jewish rabbi's had been teaching for years—this confused them even more. And this is why it is so hard for the majority of professed Christians today to accept what I am saying as God's truths. We today, as the Jews then, have been taught so many different things over the years that what I am telling you doesn't sound even half right. But, instead of checking these things out, the majority of people will automatically reject these truths just as most Jews rejected Jesus as their promised Messiah.

After Jesus rose from the tomb and was caught up to God, the afflictions and persecutions only worsened for the new Christian believers as they stepped out onto the world scene. They not only had the Romans to contend with but the Jews also. (See Romans 8:19-27, 2 Timothy 3:12-15, and 1 John 3:1-3.)

Verses 3 and 4 of Revelation 12 refer to Satan, the accuser of the children of God from the beginning of time. He and his evil imps also knew that Jesus' birth was at hand just as they know His second coming is near at hand. Diligently they worked (and are working and will work) through corrupt religious and governmental leaders who went about (and are going about) blinding the eyes of God's people by making God's Holy Word a burden instead of the joy it was meant to be. Satan had for years subtly worked through the governmental powers such as Babylon, Egypt, Persia, Assyria, Greece, and Pagan Rome, as well as their own religious leaders of Papal Rome (which is identified by the "seven heads"), and he will continue to work into the future until he and his evil army are taken out of the way.

We find in Matthew 2:16 what has been referred to as "the massacre of the innocents"—"Then Herod, when he saw that he was mocked of the wise men, was exceeding wroth, and sent forth, and slew all the children that were in Bethlehem, and in all the coasts thereof, from two years old and under, according to the time which he had diligently inquired of the wise men." Also, read verses 17-18, which will refer you to Jeremiah 31:15. This tells of Rachel's weeping for her children.

Looking back at Revelation 12:6,10, 11, and 16, we discover that these verses refer to the New Testament church through what we call the dark ages (from AD 538 through AD 1798, an exact period of 1260 years, as predicted in Daniel 7:25, 12:7; and Revelation 11:2-3, 12:6, 12:14, 13:5)—a time when it was forbidden by the popes of the Roman Catholic Church, each in their succession, for any person to have in their possession, whole or in part, any Bible verse. The penalty if caught was death. And although the Christians of that time tried to escape into the mountains and hide, it is estimated that between 75 and 100 million men, women, and children were tracked down and put to death during that fearful time simply because they refused to follow the dictates of the Roman Catholic Church.

The rest of this chapter tells of the struggle between Satan and God's people and how, only through their faith in Jesus, will the remnant church "which keep the commandments of God and have the testimony of Jesus Christ" at last win the victory (verse 17).

Now, while most preachers teach that verse 17 speaks of two separate groups—the Jews as a nation and the Christians—I beg to differ. This same statement is repeated in Revelation 14:12, which says, "Here is the patience of the saints: here are they that keep the commandments of God, and the faith of Jesus."

Think of this for a moment. If these two verses were speaking of two separate groups, verse 17 would be worded like this: those that keep the commandments of God, and those who have the testimony of Jesus Christ. And Revelation 14:12 would be worded like this: they that keep the commandments of God, and those who have the faith of Jesus.

A careful examination of the verses tells us that this is not what these two verses are saying at all. Both are speaking of one group of people: those who "keep the commandments of God [all ten], and have the testimony of Jesus Christ" (Revelation 12:17). In John 10:16 we read, "And other sheep I have, which are not of this fold [meaning these 'other sheep' are not Jews]: them also I must bring, and they shall hear my voice; and there shall be one fold, and one shepherd [one fold = one group / one shepherd = one Lord]." Am I right?

THE WOMAN RIDING
THE BEAST

In Revelation 17 we find a much different woman. Instead of trying to explain each verse myself, I will present verses 1 through 7 and then give you the story while allowing God's Word to interpret itself as God designed it to do.

- "And there came one of the seven angels which had the seven vials, and talked with me, saying unto me, Come hither; I will shew unto thee the judgment of the great whore that sitteth upon many waters" (verse 1). (Check also Jeremiah 51:13.)

- "With whom the kings of the earth have committed fornication, and the inhabitants of the earth have been made drunk with the wine of her fornication" (verse 2).

- "So he carried me away in the spirit into the wilderness: and I saw a woman sit upon a scarlet coloured beast, full of names of blasphemy, having seven heads and ten horns" (verse 3).

- "And the woman was arrayed in purple and scarlet

colour, and decked with gold and precious stones and pearls, having a golden cup in her hand full of abominations and filthiness of her fornication" (verse 4).

- "And upon her forehead was a name written, MYSTERY, BABYLON THE GREAT, THE MOTHER OF HARLOTS AND ABOMINATIONS OF THE EARTH" (verse 5).

- "And I saw a woman drunken with the blood of the saints, and with the blood of the martyrs of Jesus: and when I saw her, I wondered with great admiration" (verse 6).

- "And the angel said unto me, Wherefore dist thou marvel? I will tell thee the mystery of the woman, and of the beast that carrieth her, which hath the seven heads and ten horns" (verse 7).

Beginning at verse 8 we have God's interpretation of this vision. Just as God had done with Daniel (see Daniel 7), He also did with John. That way when the time comes, the old excuse of "I did not understand" won't be good enough. God explains everything down to the last period. It is all right there in front of us in black and white. All we have to do is read it. God tells us in Amos 3:7: "Surely the Lord GOD will do nothing, but he revealeth his secret unto his servants the prophets." (Check also Genesis 6:13 and John 15:15.) All we as servants of God and followers of His Son Jesus Christ have to do is accept the Bible as the holy, inspired Word of God. This is the reason I asked at the beginning of this study if you totally believe the Bible as truth.

As I have said before, this woman represents a worldwide church system that has had and even now has (although her power is veiled in secrecy) the last word in all religious and secular matters. This is shown by her riding astride the beast. She's in control. And by force (not by her own power), she has brought almost the whole world under her control. Those who refuse to bow in submission have and will be taken out of the way. Kings and nations have done her bidding. The world has been made drunk with her intoxicating teachings. The colors she wears only make it easier for us to identify her. These same colors were worn by the priest of ancient Babylon and are now worn by the popes, cardinals, bishops, and priests of the Roman Catholic Church. I know some are saying there are some Protestant churches whose preachers wear similar colors, and that is true. But they do not meet the specifications given to identify and locate this beast. I will say more about those specifications in the next part of this study.

An interesting tidbit to inject here is that in the jubilee year of 1825 Pope Leo XII had a special cup made to commemorate the event. On one side of the cup, he had his own image engraved, while on the opposite side he had an image of a woman engraved. In her left hand, she held a cross; in her right hand, she held a cup. Around her was an inscription that read in Latin, "Sedet Super Universum"; when translated into English, it reads "the whole world is her seat." Strange coincidence? I think not. God's Holy Word gave us this information concerning this woman, and there it is.

Now remember, the Bible in its original text had no chapters or verses. This was done much later for easy referencing. And taking this into consideration, we find that the next couple of verses have a double application, because they are repeated several times in slightly different terms. Which as you will see is a history of this "beast" that will somehow be in control of the whole world during the end time or in other words at the time of our Lord's second coming.

You will see what I mean as we take a closer look at this

next verse. To enable us to come to an easy understanding of the highly symbolic language of this verse, I will print the verse in full then split it up into small portions so we can digest it a little at a time.

"The beast that thou sawest was, and is not; and shall ascend out of the bottomless pit, and go into perdition: and they that dwell on the earth shall wonder, whose names were not written in the book of life from the foundation of the world, when they behold the beast that was, and is not, and yet is" (verse 8).

The first four words, "the beast that was," directs our attention to the old pagan Roman Empire which Satan worked through in order to persecute the new Christian sect which was beginning to form just after AD 34. The next three words, "and is not," directs us to the period when the old Roman Empire (during the reign of Constantine who claimed to have had a vision from heaven) seemed to have been transformed into a Christian nation just before it broke up into the ten nation confederation and, therefore, was no longer persecuting Christians. Over time the old Roman Empire broke into the ten nation confederation (of which three of those ten nations were overthrown because they each refused to bow to the dictates of their papal dictators).

After those three nations were taken out of the way, we have the next eight words, "and shall ascend out of the bottomless pit." This refers to the papacy's rise to world domination as The Holy Roman Empire during the 1260 years from AD 538 thru AD 1798 (which I spoke of a few pages back) and the new persecuting power of not only the Christians but of any nation and or people in the whole known world who would not bow to its dictates. The next four words, "and go into perdition," direct us to the final destruction of this false religious system at Jesus' second coming.

Then we have this center section that divides the two stages of the progress of this beast. Let's look at the next 38 words, and you will see the second application is but a continuation of the same thought: "And they that dwell on the earth shall wonder, whose names were not written in the book of life from the foundation of the world, when they behold the beast that was, and is not, and yet is."

Now, ask yourself these three questions:

1. Who else in the whole world would be wondering if their names are written in the book of life but those who profess to be Christians? To find out what book they're speaking of check Exodus 32:33, which says, "And the Lord said unto Moses, Whosoever hath sinned against me, him will I blot out of my book."

2. What worldwide church system claims to be the "mother church" whose head man claims "he sits in the place of God" and claims to have the power to forgive sin or if need be can excommunicate even the angels of heaven? Everyone should know it is the popes of the Roman Catholic Church who have in the past and in the present and will in the future make this claim.

3. What worldwide church system came into power as the old Roman Empire crumbled into the dust? Look to the history books printed before 1970; they will tell you it was the Roman Catholic Church.

By knowing these things, we find "the beast that was" has to be directing our attention toward a worldwide church/state system that rose out of the ashes of the old Roman Empire to become a world power that not only would dominate the world but also persecute all those who refused to go along with its dictates (for the 1260 years), which as history has proven, the Roman Catholic Church did that from AD 538 through AD 1798. You do the math.

The "and was not" refers to the papacies lose of power on February 20, 1798, when Napoleon sent General Berthier to take Pope Pius VI prisoner. The "and shall ascend out of the bottomless pit" refers to 1929 when Mussolini executed what is known as "The Concordat of 1929," which reinstated all of the papacy's powers and lands. At that time, the Roman Catholic Church slowly but surely began regaining its power until once again it has become a world power unto itself. Every day thousands of diplomats go in and out of the Vatican from almost every nation around the world seeking advice.

The "and go into perdition" refers to the total destruction of not only this false religious system but also all those who either believe or in some way go along with its lies. This next verse points to the location of this worldwide religious/secular church system.

Revelation 17:9 says, "And here is the mind which hath wisdom. The seven heads are seven mountains, on which the woman sitteth." (Check Revelation 13:1-8.) As I stated a few pages back, this verse without a doubt is pointing to no other geographical location on earth but the seven hills of Rome.

Moving on to verse 10: "And there are seven kings: five are fallen, and one is, and the other is not yet come; and when he cometh, he must continue a short space." The main thing to remember is that this is a continuing prophecy which begins at the new beginning of the papacy (1929) and ends with the second coming of our Lord Jesus Christ. So carefully consider the following. From the time Mussolini executed "The Concordat of 1929," which reinstated all powers and lands to the Roman Catholic Church, there have been six popes. The five that have fallen are Popes Pius XI,

1922-1939; Pius XII, 1939-1958; John XXIII, 1958-1963; Paul VI, 1963-1978; John Paul I, 1978; John Paul II 1978-2005. So the "and one is" can only be pointing to John Paul II who was the most traveled pope in history. Never before in the history of the papacy has any pope been able to go to even half of the countries that John Paul II did.

Then we read "and the other is not yet come; and when he cometh, he must continue a short space." So this present pope (Benedict) is the seventh king (or pope) because John Paul II was the sixth, and he will continue where John Paul II left off. But, as we see he will not reign for very long before another will take his place.

Verse 11 says, "And the beast that was, and is not, even he is the eighth, and is of the seven, and goeth into perdition." The first portion of this verse—"And the beast that was, and is not"—refers to the time when the Holy Roman Empire lost its power. But God wants to be sure we understand that no matter how good this last pope's intentions may seem, he is still connected to this same beast. We are told "even he is the eighth, and is of the seven, and goeth into perdition." This refers to the last pope who will be reigning at the time of Jesus' second coming when this worldwide church system shall be utterly destroyed along with the rest of the world's population after Jesus has rescued His elect out of harm's way. There have been some who claim this last pope will be a manifestation of Satan himself.

Many ask, "Why all these riddles?" Well, we find the answer to this question in Matthew 13:10-17. The disciples came to Jesus and asked this same question. Jesus' answer was simple and to the point. In verse 11 we read, "He answered and said unto them, Because it is given unto you to know the mysteries of the kingdom of heaven, but to them it is not given." Then, in verse 15 we read, "For this people's heart is waxed gross, and their ears are dull of hearing, and their eyes they have closed; least at any time they should see with their eyes and hear with their ears, and should understand with their heart, and should be converted, and I should heal them." (Check also Mark 4:10-12.)

No matter what, there will be many who will read these truths and plainly see for themselves from the Bible that what I am saying is true but will reject these things because it is not what they have been taught over the years by preachers and Bible teachers of the mainstream religions of the day. This is why Jesus repeated these things so many times throughout His ministry. That way when the time comes to chose, each of us will be held accountable for our choice.

The next three verses of Revelation 17 fit together in that they describe a complete event.

- "And the ten horns which thou sawest are ten kings, which have received no kingdom as yet; but received power as kings one hour with the beast" (verse 12).
- "These have one mind, and shall give their power and strength unto the beast" (verse 13).
- "These shall make war with the Lamb, and the Lamb shall overcome them: for he is Lord of lords, and King of kings: and they that are with him are called, and chosen, and faithful" (verse 14).

The beast spoken of here and the beast of Daniel 7:7 and 20-26 direct our attention once again to the breakup of the old Roman Empire into ten nations. At first, the ten nations gave their full support to the papacy until they saw that the papacy was controlling them instead of them controlling it. One by one each nation was either overthrown or it capitulated their power to the will of the papacy. It not only happened then but it will happen again just before Jesus' second coming as you will see in the last part of this study—The Image of the Beast. (Check 2 Thessalonians 2:1-12.)

The next few pages are a study of ancient history as it agrees and matches Bible prophecy of end time events.

BABYLON THE GREAT

In Revelation 17:4-6 we are given a description or comparison of what the end time apostate church will be like just before Jesus' second coming.

We read in verses 4-6: "And the woman was arrayed in purple and scarlet colour, and decked with gold and precious stones and pearls, having a golden cup in her hand full of abominations and filthiness of her fornication: And upon her forehead was a name written, MYSTERY, BABYLON THE GREAT, THE MOTHER OF HARLOTS AND ABOMINATIONS OF THE EARTH. And I saw the woman drunken with the blood of the saints, and with the blood of the martyrs of Jesus; and when I saw her, I wondered with great admiration."

No one should misunderstand the description given in verse 4 because all one has to do is look for a worldwide church system whose priest wear those colors and whose teachings are contrary to God's Holy Word.

Remembering that, most of the terms in verses 5 and 6 are symbolic. Verse 5 is telling us that this church will somehow connect with ancient Babylon while verse 6 is showing us that this church is drunk with power, and all those who do not submit to her authority will be thrown into prison and killed. The reason John "wondered with great admiration" was because he could not understand how this supposed church of God's could be so terrifying, cruel, and unyielding.

A quick point here: if you will turn to Hosea 2:5, you will find one of many references where God referred to Israel as a harlot because they once again started worshipping other gods (or idols) and had forsaken God's laws (the Ten Commandments). We also see that man's ideas and teachings of God's love and grace is contrary to what God's Holy Word says.

In Hosea 4:6 we read, "My people are destroyed for lack of knowledge: because thou hast rejected knowledge, I will also reject thee, that thou shalt be no priest to me: seeing thou hast forgotten the law of thy God, I will also forget thy children."

Also, check Deuteronomy 4:23-31. Following is Deuteronomy 28:9: "The LORD shall establish thee an holy people unto himself, as he hath sworn unto thee, [here are the conditions] if thou shalt keep the commandments of the LORD thy God, and walk in his ways." Verse 13 repeats these same conditions; verse 45 makes these conditions a little clearer. See also Deuteronomy 30:14-20. Verse 15 reads, "See, I have set before thee this day life and good, and death and evil." The final decision is left to the individual. The questions are: Will you choose life by hearing and obeying God's Word? Or will you choose death by hearing and obeying man's interpretation of God's Word?

We are told in Revelation 16:19, "And the great city was divided into three parts, and the cities of the nations fell: and great Babylon came in remembrance before God, to give unto her the cup of wine of the fierceness of his wrath."

It is true that God was speaking only to the nation of Israel at this particular time, but if you have read my study "The Lost Ten Tribes of Israel? Or Where Is Abraham's Seed" then you already know this statement refers now to the whole world.

By taking the aforementioned descriptions into consideration I believe it is reasonable to assume this end time Babylon will resemble ancient Babylon. So, let's go to the history books—*The Story of Civilization* by Will Durant—and see what ancient Babylon was like.

We are told that Babylon was situated majestically near the banks of both the Tigris and Euphrates rivers in what was known as lower Mesopotamia. Babylon was the Eden of Semitic legend—a product of the Akkadian and Sumerian peoples with the Akkadians being the dominant strain. King Hammurabi, who reigned from 2123-2081 BC, ruled over the area. As a conquering genius, no one was his equal. By force he set about bringing the smaller nations and kingdoms under his control. Once his troops set siege against a nation it is said they had but two choices: be wiped off the face of the earth or surrender and join him against others. He overthrew every nation except the Kassites. (I will say more on them in a little while.)

As a law giver he was extraordinary. In 1902 near Susa a beautifully engraved diorite cylinder was unearthed by archeologist known as The Code of Hammurabi. The cylinder had been taken to Elam as a trophy of war around 1100 BC. On one side of the cylinder was an engraved picture showing King Hammurabi receiving the laws from Shamash the Sun-god. I will paraphrase the caption which proclaimed, "Anu, King of the Anunaki, Bel, Lord of Heaven and Earth and Marduk ruler over all mankind has established Babylon as an everlasting kingdom and has set and exalted King Hammurabi to rule in our place." On the other side were written 285 laws under the heading "The righteous laws which Hammurabi the wise king established. I am the guardian governor."

King Hammurabi had temples built for Marduk and his wife, whose name is not mentioned in history, plus many other lesser gods. The empire became the wealthiest empire up to that point. The people learned how to use dye and began dying their cloth. They also began wearing sandals instead of going barefoot, and they developed a taste for hair ornaments, necklaces, bracelets, and amulets. But, as most people of wealth, they began to enjoy their luxury and peace too much and became soft and forgot the art of war. What had been the strongest army in the world was quickly reduced to almost nothing. And this is what the Kassites had long waited for.

Just across Babylon's furthest eastern boundary the warring mountain tribe known as the Kassites had for years looked with envy upon all the riches of Babylon. Eight years after King Hammurabi's death, they swarmed down like locust and quickly plundered the land. Then they retreated back to the safety of their mountains. After a little time had passed, they raided Babylon again, then again. Once the people could no longer fend them off, the Kassites moved down and settled as conquerors and ruled Babylon according to their laws. They put a stop to all studies of science and art. But the Kassites were not to be the permanent residents of this kingdom. Once again they, as the Akkadians before them, enjoyed their wealth and luxurious living. And after almost 600 years of rule, the kingdom of Assyria overthrew and took charge of Babylon. It is said that when the Babylonians tried to rebel, King Sennacherib destroyed

Babylon almost completely, but King Esarhaddon stepped in and restored it to its prosperity and culture.

As time passed the Medes grew in power while the Assyrians power slowly slipped away. King Nabopolassar saw his chance—he liberated Babylon by force and set up an independent dynasty. As he lay dying, he bequeathed the Babylonian kingdom to his son Nebuchadnezzar II. One of the diorite cylinders they found was this king's address to his subjects. As he stepped up to claim his kingdom, he said, "At thy command, O merciful Marduk, may the house that I have built endure forever, may I be saturated with its splendor, attain old age therein with abundant offspring, and receive therein tribute of the kings of all regions from all mankind."

We know both from world history and Bible history that King Nebuchadnezzar's power grew and grew until he was the most powerful ruler on earth. Most accounts claim him to be a fierce warrior, able statesman, and builder of all the kings and rulers before him. But there came a time when Egypt and Assyria conspired together to overthrow Babylon, and if it had been anyone besides Nebuchadnezzar, their joint effort may have been pulled off.

We are told through uncovered documents that Nebuchadnezzar mustered his forces and met the combined Egyptian/Assyrian force at a place called Carchemish, which was located on the upper Euphrates River, and almost annihilated them. Once they had surrendered, Palestine and all of Syria fell easily under his sway. Babylonian merchants controlled all trade across western Asia, from the Persian Gulf to the Mediterranean Sea. The proceeds from the tolls, tributes, and taxes that Nebuchadnezzar received were spent on beautifying and building Babylon until it became the largest, most magnificent metropolis of the ancient world. Its most memorable structures were the Tower of Babel, which stood some 650 feet, and the Hanging Gardens, also known as one of the seven wonders of the ancient world.

Herodotus, the Greek historian who was there and saw the city after its completion, described it this way: "It stands as a spacious plain, surrounded by a wall fifty six miles in length on either side, it stands 335 feet tall and 85 feet in width, which enclosed an area of some two hundred square miles, so broad that four, four horse chariots could be driven along the top with ease, and still left room for spectators along one side." Most of the buildings were made of brick, each having the inscription "I am Nebuchadnezzar, King of Babylon."

Many canals ran throughout the city supplying drinking water for the people and livestock and providing irrigation for the many fruit orchards and vegetable fields. To say the least, Babylon was self contained and needed no help from outside sources.

Now, let's take a quick look at the religious practices of this ancient Babylonian kingdom. To begin with, each king was crowned only after he was approved by the high priest. This was done after he dressed himself in priestly vestments and carried an image of Marduk openly through the streets. This was to symbolize he was under the rule of the priest, which simply means that Babylon was a theocratic kingdom. In other words, the religious leaders in effect ruled Babylon.

It was the high priest who chose what wars were to be fought and how much tribute the smaller nations as well as the citizens were to pay. Tribute could be anything from gold, silver, cooper, corn, or fruits or practically anything that was abundantly produced by the nation or individual paying the tribute. It was the law that the first and best of all things received as tribute went to the temples. When there was a war with another nation, the priest got first pick of all slaves, animals, or other spoils won. If, however, any nation or citizen could not pay tribute or taxes, all their lands and or possessions would became the property of the temple. As a result of this, the priests became the greatest financiers of the nation. They owned vast tracts of land and more slaves than anyone—of which they would rent to those who did not own any. The slaves who held the knowledge of a certain trade such as woodworking, stone cutting, etc., would be put to work in the temple or on the temple grounds, because the priests ran their own shops and sold incense, candles, statues, prayer cloths, charms, and many other such things.

The priests were also the lawyers of that day. For a price, they drew up contracts, wills, held trials, and decided the outcome of law suits; they also kept track of all official records such as birth and death records, buying livestock, and any number of other commercial transactions. In fact, some of the priests had so much power that they could actually dethrone the king if he did not agree with their decision. The priest named their power "the advantage of prominence" simply because the king would sooner or later die, while the gods lived forever.

And speaking of gods, these people worshipped many, many gods. In fact, archeologists claim they have unearthed some 800 statues, plaques, and prayer cloths, which depicted certain gods with inscriptions that told what help each god was supposed to perform. These statues, plaques, and prayer cloths were placed on walls, floors, in windows, on door facings from room to room, and in yards, both on the ground and hanging from trees. These 800 artifacts were unearthed just from Babylon alone. The count sores to a whopping 65,000 with the digs in and around the towns and villages throughout the crescent valley. Some were thought of as great deities, most were lesser deities. As if they didn't have enough gods of their own, some had been adopted from Egypt and other surrounding nations. Each town, village, and province had a multitude of both gods and goddesses whom they believed not only watched over them but protected them from other gods. There were house gods, crop gods, road gods, rain gods, wind gods, water gods—the list goes on.

They believed some of these gods took on the form of animals such as bulls, rams, hawks, falcons or other birds, cows, cats, crocodiles, goats, chickens, jackals, or even snakes. The gods did this so they could live on earth near their subjects who praised and worshipped them. Most of these animals were allowed to freely roam through the temples as the cow does today in India, just to give one example. Women were drugged, then tied to alters, and offered to these animal gods for sexual mates.

But out of all these gods and goddesses there were two that were elevated above all the others. These two were Marduk and Ishtor—Ishtor had been known as Isis in Egypt; Astrarte, Aphrodite, or Venus to the Greeks; Cybele in Asia; and Easter to the Romans. All these were the same goddess; her name was just spelled and pronounced differently. She was even given her own day, which was referred to as Easter's Day. During the time of Jesus, it was celebrated on the second Sunday of the Jewish month of Nisan, which corresponds with the fourth Sunday of our April. Today, in America we celebrate it as Easter Sunday. Since Isis was the mother of Horus, the sun god, she was called the mother of god who created all things. She was also known as the queen of heaven. (Check Jeremiah 7:15-19, 23-24; 8:1-3, 19; 18:12-13; 19:11-13.)

It was the same with Isis's son, Horus, the sun god, who was also known as Marduk, Osiris, Tammuz, Adonis, Moloch,

Mithra, Bacchus, Isvara, Deoius, Jupiter, Plutus, Ninus, Dionysus, Iacchus, Ittis; the names he was known as could go on and on, but I believe you get the picture. Horus was reportedly born on December 25, representing the rebirth of the sun. As the pagan god-child, he was called Baal-berith, which translated means lord of the fir-tree. The word Yule is a Babylonian word for infant. December 25 was called Yule Day by the pagan Anglo-Saxons. The Persian sun god Mithra, which means lord, was widely accepted and worshipped in the Roman world prior to the period of Christian evangelism. (Check Acts 17:16-24.) Sunday was dedicated to Mithra, and Sunday received the title of the lord's day from the pagan world.

Many statues were found that had been made of clay or carved from wood, and drawings were found showing Isis or Ishtar holding her baby son, Horus, which she reportedly conceived as a virgin, in her arms. It was believed she could intercede for her devoted followers when her son, Horus, became angry with something they had done. She was known as the goddess of both love and war and the goddess of fertility—many believed she roamed the earth as a female rabbit since rabbits reproduced so abundantly.

Figuring themselves sole spokesmen for their gods, the priests proclaimed themselves infallible. During the actual worship service, they made use of a small round wafer that they claimed was the body of their god Horus. Also, they used bells, prayer beads, and incense, and they carried relics and images through the temples and along the streets on certain days of the year of which the lord's day, December 25, was the most holy with Easter Sunday coming in a close second.

After learning this much information about the worshipping habits of ancient Babylon, is it any wonder why God referred to this end time mother church as Babylon? Now, I ask you, in the world today, what worldwide religion would you say parallels the descriptions I have given of ancient Babylon?

So, without hesitation let's begin the last part of this study.

THE IMAGE OF
THE BEAST

To begin with I would like to ask a question. What is an image? The *Dictionary of the English Language* tells us that an image is "a reproduction of the appearance of someone or something; especially, a sculptured likeness. An optically formed duplicate, counterpart or other representative reproduction of an object; especially an optical reproduction of an object formed by a lens or mirror."

We already know from previous pages that each of these beasts represent a different kingdom or nation. So common sense dictates that the next beast we find in Revelation 13:11-17 is another nation. But we see right away that it is a different kind of nation than any before it. We also see that this nation comes up just as the previous beast, or nation, of verse 10, the one that ruled the world for 1260 years or from AD 538-1798 goes into captivity. Let's take a closer look at verse 11: "And I beheld another beast coming up out of the earth; and he had two horns like a lamb, and he spake as a dragon."

History tells us that the only nation that was "coming up" at that time was the United States of America, and America meets the description given in the first eleven words. I say this because the beast before it rose "up out of the sea" which, as we found in Revelation 17:15, represents "peoples, and multitudes, and nations, and tongues"—which could have only been the continent of Europe.

So, the idea of this particular beast "coming up out of the earth" has to be a nation coming up "as a lamb" in a virtually unpopulated, dense part of the world—a land unlike the crowded nations of Europe where religious intolerance continued to oppress the people; a land where the people could be free to choose their destiny for themselves instead of having it chosen for them.

The next seven words, "and had two horns like a lamb," cause some people a bit of trouble when they try to figure them out. I believe the main reason for this is the fact that not very many people know that this verse is speaking specifically of the United States of America. But, by knowing this now, think for a moment, and you will see how those seven words are a perfect fit to the description of the early, youthful days of America. I remind you of the first paragraph of the Constitution of the United States: "We the people of the United States, in Order to form a more perfect Union, establish Justice, insure domestic Tranquility, provide for the common defense, promote the general Welfare, and secure the Blessings of Liberty to ourselves and our Posterity, do ordain and establish this Constitution of the United States of America."

Simply put, the power of the government comes from the people who rule the government not from the church who had ruled both the government and the people back in the Old World, Europe.

The first sixteen words in the First Amendment of the Bill of Rights state, "Congress shall make no law respecting an establishment of religion, or prohibiting the free exercise thereof." Concerning the formation of this nation, Mr. J.A. Bingham stated it this way about the new nation: "a church without a pope and a state without a king."

Our forefathers wanted a place where they could form a democratic government that would allow them to have a say in how it was being run and a place where they could worship as their conscious dictated. You see, my friend, their idea was to keep a separation between religion and government. But we also find that something goes terribly wrong, because when we look at the last six words of verse 11, we read, "and he spake as a dragon."

So we must ask ourselves, how does a nation speak? And the answer is simple. A nation speaks through its legislative body. Every time a new law is passed, the nation has spoken. So we can conclude that either a law or laws will be passed that will make the United States become a persecuting power. What law or group of laws could do this? Well, we are given a couple of clues in the next verse.

Verse 12 states, "And he exerciseth all the power of the first beast before him, and causeth the earth and them which dwell therein to worship the first beast, whose deadly wound was healed."

We already know the beast just before this one was the Roman Catholic Church whose deadly wound was healed when Mussolini executed "The Concordat Of 1929," which restored all the power and properties to the papacy. But those fourteen words in the center of this verse tell us what we need to know. And that is that the law or laws which will be passed will have something to do with how we worship. This not only ties this beast back with the Roman Catholic

Church, which the framers of this great nation fought so hard to escape, but it also ties this last beast back into the Babylonian religion. When this happens, this last beast, the United States, will become what is referred to in Revelation 19:20 as "the false prophet." Read the center part of Revelation 13:12, and you will see what I mean: "and causeth the earth and them which dwell therein to worship the first beast."

Don't give up on me now. I assure you it will all come together in just a little while. Let's look back to Daniel 3:4-15 and 6:10-12, 16. I will paraphrase since it is such a long passage. Nebuchadnezzar, the king of Babylon, had a golden image erected and invited all the high-ranking people from all over his kingdom to come to its dedication. He sent out the town crier to inform everyone that when they heard certain music being played everyone must bow down and worship the image. And, if anyone did not bow down, they would be thrown into a fiery furnace.

So, when all had gathered and the music began to play, everyone bowed down and worshipped the golden image. Everyone that is except three young Hebrews named Shadrach, Meshach, and Abednego. Right away they were spotted, arrested, and brought before the king. To say the least, King Nebuchadnezzar was angry with them, but he was willing to give these three men another chance. After all, they may not have gotten the memo.

"Now if ye be ready that at what time ye hear the sound of the . . . musick, ye fall down and worship the image which I have made; well: but if ye worship not, ye shall be cast the same hour into the midst of a burning fiery furnace; and who is that God that shall deliver you out of my hands?" (Daniel 3:15).

We are told in verses 16-18 that their answer was quick and to the point: "Shadrach, Meshach, and Abednego, answered and said to the king, O Nebuchadnezzar, we are not careful to answer thee in this mater. If it be so, our God whom we serve is able to deliver us from the burning fiery furnace, and he will deliver us out of thine hand, O king. But if not, be it known unto thee, O king, that we will not serve thy gods, nor worship the golden image which thou hast set up."

To say the least, King Nebuchadnezzar was very angry at their answer and commanded that the furnace be heated seven times hotter than hot. Then, he had the guards bind them and throw them into the middle of the fire in the furnace. We are told that the fire was so hot that it killed the guards who threw these three Hebrew men into the furnace. After a few moments had passed, King Nebuchadnezzar looked into the flames and was amazed at what he saw.

"Then Nebuchadnezzar . . . said unto his counselors, Did not we cast three men bound into the midst of the fire? They answered and said unto the king, True, O king. He answered and said, Lo, I see four men loose, walking in the midst of the fire, and they have no hurt; and the form of the fourth is like the Son of God" (verses 24-25).

Going a little closer to the mouth of the furnace, the king said, "Shadrach, Meshach, and Abednego, ye servants of the most high God, come forth, and come hither" (verse 26).

And when they had come out of the fire, everyone gathered around to look at these amazing men. Not a hair on their head was singed nor was the smell of the fire on their coats. I tell you, my dear friend, we serve an amazing God.

Then, we read in Daniel 6:8-23 that King Darius of Babylon had Daniel thrown into the lions' den because he would not bow down and worship the king as everyone had been instructed to do. Instead, Daniel continued to worship the God of heaven who created the heavens and the earth and all things that are in them. But the next morning when King Darius came to the lions' den and commanded the guards to remove the stone from atop the hole, he found that God had shut the mouths of the lions, and Daniel was alive and not hurt.

In Acts 5:17-33 we read of how Peter and a couple of the apostles had been thrown into prison for preaching the gospel. During the night an angel of the Lord brought them forth from the prison and told them to go to the temple and preach. And when the guards were sent to bring the apostles before the priest, it was found that they were no longer in prison as they were supposed to be. Someone came and told the priest that the men were in the temple preaching.

When the apostles were finally brought before him, the priest did not ask how they had gotten out of prison without even being seen, instead he asked, "Did not we straitly command you that ye should not teach in this name? and, behold, ye have filled Jerusalem with your doctrine, and intend to bring this man's blood upon us. Then Peter and the other apostles answered and said, We ought to obey God rather than man. The God of our fathers raised up Jesus, whom ye slew and hanged on a tree. Him hath God exalted with his right hand to be a Prince and Saviour, for to give repentance to Israel, and forgiveness of sins. And we are his witnesses of these things; and so is also the Holy Ghost, whom God hath given to them that obey him" (Acts 5:28-32).

In Revelation 1:9 we read, "I John, who also am your brother, and companion in tribulation, and in the kingdom and patience of Jesus Christ, was in the isle that is called Patmos, for the word of God, and for the testimony of Jesus Christ."

I have presented the stories of these godly men because I want to ask you another question. What crimes did these men commit? Were they punished because they refused to worship according to man's form of religion? In spite of persecution, they were prepared to give their lives; and through the ages millions of Christians have been persecuted rather than compromise God's Holy Word.

In the next couple of verses we find strange events taking place. Let's take a closer look, shall we? In Revelation 13:13-14 we read, "And he doeth great wonders, so that he maketh fire come down from heaven on the earth in the sight of men, And deceiveth them that dwell on the earth by the means of those miracles which he had power to do in the sight of the beast; saying to them that dwell on the earth, that they should make an image to the beast, which had the wound by a sword, and did live,"

These two verses boggle the mind when trying to discern their meaning. The reason for this is because we look for our answers in the natural world. But if we search God's Holy Scriptures, as we are instructed to do, we would find answers for these riddles. Unfortunately, since these answers are found in the unnatural world, many people will not accept them because people want things they can see with their eyes, hold in their hands, smell with their noses, or taste in their mouths. Although these unnatural things of God's are mentioned hundreds of times throughout the Bible, very few professed Christians believe they can happen or that they ever happened.

In 2 Corinthians 11:11-15 we read of men and women who falsely claimed they were prophets, healers, preachers, or teachers of the gospel of Jesus Christ. Just as there are people today who are falsely claiming to receive visions or words of knowledge directly from God. Millions of deluded people flock to the meetings held by these false ministers, never believing for an instant it is not God's Holy Spirit who is at work amongst them.

The apostle Paul tells us in verse 13-15 of that chapter, "For such are false apostles, deceitful workers, transforming themselves into the apostles of Christ. And no marvel; for Satan himself is transformed into an angel of light. Therefore it is no great thing if his ministers also be transformed as the ministers of righteousness; whose end shall be according to their works."

In Ephesians 6:11-13 we are once again instructed by Paul to "put on the whole armour of God, that ye may be able to stand against the wiles of the devil. For we wrestle not against flesh and blood, but against principalities, against powers, against the rulers of darkness of this world, against spiritual wickedness in high places. Wherefore take unto you the whole armour of God, that you may be able to withstand in the evil day, and having done all, to stand."

Even more, Jesus spoke of end time events in Matthew 24:23-26: "Then if any man shall say unto you, Lo, here is Christ, or there; believe it not. For there shall arise false Christs, and false prophets, and shall shew great signs and wonders; insomuch that, if it were possible, they shall deceive the very elect. Behold, I have told you before. Wherefore if they shall say unto you, Behold, he is in the desert; go not forth: behold, he is in the secret chambers; believe it not."

I believe that it is safe for us to conclude that these verses are directing us to watch who we listen to. There are many in the world today who go about teaching false doctrines or claiming to be able to perform miraculous healings and miracles or to have received some new revelation. Then there are those who claim to be able to communicate with the dead, but I will leave that for another study.

Jesus stated in Matthew 7:21-23: "Not every one that saith unto me, Lord, Lord, shall enter into the kingdom of heaven; but he that doeth the will of my Father which is in heaven. Many will say to me in that day, Lord, Lord, have we not prophesied in thy name? and in thy name have cast out devils? and in thy name done many wonderful works? And then will I profess unto them, I never knew you: depart from me, ye that work iniquity." These same things were going on while Jesus was walking about teaching God's truths.

Just a few years after Jesus had risen from the tomb, Paul wrote: "I marvel that ye are so soon removed from him that called you into the grace of Christ unto another gospel: Which is not another; but there be some that trouble you, and would pervert the gospel of Christ" (Galatians 1:6-7).

This ties in with what I was saying a few pages back about the "false prophet." It is plain to see that Paul is talking about those who are preaching the gospel but in some way perverting it by changing a few things so people won't think bad of them for telling it like it is.

We find in 2 Timothy 4:1-4 more advice: "I charge thee therefore before God, and the Lord Jesus Christ, who shall judge the quick and the dead at his appearing and his kingdom; Preach the word; be instant in season, out of season; reprove, rebuke, exhort with all long-suffering and doctrine. For the time will come when they will not endure sound doctrine; but after their own lusts shall they heap to themselves teachers, having itching ears; And they shall turn away their ears from the truth, and shall be turned unto fables." This is the time we live in today. If you try to lead people through a study of God's Word, most people only want to talk about what this or that preacher says about this or that. Most people don't want to hear God's truths; all they want to hear is I'm OK, your OK.

At this we must ask ourselves, how can we tell if a prophet is truly speaking for God or not? Let's read Isaiah

8:20: "To the law and to the testimony: if they speaking not according to this word [the Bible], it is because there is no light [truth] in them." Then, in 2 Timothy 3:16 it says, "All scripture is given by inspiration of God, and is profitable for doctrine, for reproof, for correction, for instruction in righteousness."

Adding to these thoughts, 2 Peter 1:20-21 says, "Knowing this first, that no prophecy of the scripture is of any private interpretation. For the prophecy came not in old time by the will of man: but holy men of God spake as they were moved by the Holy Ghost." (Read also 2 Peter 2:1-9.)

So, a true prophet, preacher, or teacher will both preach and teach God's Holy Word as it is written. Not adding or taking anything away from it. While a false prophet, preacher, or teacher will mix traditional teachings and heresies with Bible truths.

And you may ask, what heresies am I referring to? Well, allow me to list a few of the false doctrines that are being taught to God's people. And these are not only taught by the Roman Catholic Church but by Protestant churches as well; that way you can see for yourself how far from God's truths we have been led. I will begin at about the year AD 300.

- Prayers for the dead began around the year AD 300. It not only was but is being taught that for a small price the priest can and will pray a loved one out of hell.

- The exaltation of Mary began around the year AD 431. The term "mother of God" was first applied to her by the council of Ephesus. The Bible teaches us that God had no beginning, nor has any end, so how can Mary be the "mother of God"? Some will argue that this is just a term of respect. Now, while I agree that Mary was the mother of Jesus, who was and is the Son of God and or the second part of the Godhead, this does not make Mary the "mother of God."

- The kissing of the pope's feet or hand began about AD 709 by order of Pope Constantine. We are shown by example that even though the angels of heaven were created a little higher in status that humans we are not to bow down to them. We are instructed in Revelation 19:10: "And I fell at his feet to worship him. And he said unto me, See thou do it not: I am thy fellowservant, and of thy brethren that have the testimony of Jesus: worship God: for the testimony of Jesus is the spirit of prophecy."

- Church tradition is declared by the Council of Trent to be above or equal in authority to Bible teachings in 1545.

- The Syllabus of Errors was proclaimed by Pope Pius X and ratified by the First Vatican Council as the "truth of God" in 1864. This proclamation condemns freedom of religion, speech, press, and all scientific discoveries that have not been approved by the Catholic Church.

- The temporal authority of the pope over all rulers was also officially reaffirmed in 1864.

- The absolute infallibility of the pope in all matters of faith and morals was proclaimed by Vatican I council in 1870.

- The assumption of the virgin Mary was proclaimed by Pope Pius XII in 1950. They claim that Mary's body was taken to heaven shortly after her death.

There are also two other doctrines that are now being discussed by the Vatican.

- The idea of declaring Mary as the mediatrix of mankind, which simply means that God and Jesus can only be approached through *her*.

- The dogma of Mary as the coredemptrix of the world—
that man's redemption from start to finish is done through
Mary working together step by step with Christ Jesus.

You may be thinking right now, "But that is done only in
the Catholic Church, and I am not a Catholic; I am a
Protestant. So, none of these things apply to me." Well, I am
sorry but yes some of these things do apply to you. For instance, for years Protestants have been taught and most truly
believe that a second after we die, we are in heaven with
Jesus. This is not true, and those who teach this completely
disregard Bible texts that prove that this is a lie. Some
preachers have told me that although they know differently
they tell people this so they won't grieve as much.

Now, while I do agree that there are verses stating that
certain godly people were allowed an early resurrection—it
is true that Elijah was taken to heaven without even seeing
death—I assure you that everyone else is as dead and in
their graves as they were when they were placed there. But
you ask, "If our dearly departed loved ones are not with
Jesus in heaven then where are they? I will let God's Holy
Word answer that for you.

We will begin at John 5:28-29, where Jesus himself
stated, "Marvel not at this: for the hour is coming, in the
which all that are in the graves shall hear his voice, And
shall come forth; they that have done good, unto the resurrection of life; and they that have done evil, unto the resurrection of damnation." The dead are in their graves.

Then in Daniel 12:2 we read: "And many of them that
sleep in the dust of the earth shall awake, some to everlasting life, and some to shame and everlasting contempt."

As you know, Daniel was a man loved by God. But when
Daniel didn't fully understand the vision of the Lord's sec-

ond coming, as recorded in Daniel 12, he asked for clarification of the things concerning this vision, and Jesus told him in verse 13: "But go thou thy way till the end be: for thou shalt rest, and stand in thy lot at the end of the days." Daniel was going to be in the grave waiting for that shout from the Lord just like everyone else will be.

Another point I would like to inject here is that there are those who would argue with me here about the idea of Jesus talking to Daniel. But, if you would turn to Revelation 1:13-16 and compare that description with the one found in Daniel 9:5-6, there should be no doubt that it was Jesus who was talking with Daniel.

In 1 Corinthians 15:22-23 and 51-52 we read, "For as in Adam all die, even so in Christ shall all be made alive. But every man in his own order: Christ the firstfruits: afterwards they that are Christ's [now, get this part] at his coming. Behold, I shew you a mystery; We shall not all sleep [die], but we shall all be changed, In a moment, in a twinkling of an eye, at the last trump: for the trumpet shall sound, and the dead shall be raised incorruptible, and we shall be changed."

This is repeated in 1 Thessalonians 4:16-17: "For the Lord himself shall descend from heaven with a shout, with the voice of the archangel, and with the trump of God: and the dead in Christ shall rise first: Then we which are alive and remain shall be caught up together with them in the clouds, to meet the Lord in the air: and so shall we ever be with the Lord."

Looking back at the beginning of time, we find, "For dust thou art, and unto dust shalt thou return" (Genesis 3:19).

Also, in Ecclesiastes 9:5 and 10 we read, "For the living know that they shall die: but the dead know not anything, neither have they any more a reward; for the memory of them is forgotten. Whatsoever thy hand findeth to do, do it with thy might; for there is no work, nor device, nor knowledge, nor wisdom, in the grave, whither thou goest." (See also Job 7:9-10 and 14:10-15.)

I could point to other passages, but if you don't see the truth of these matters, then it is because you are refusing to accept God's Word as truth, choosing rather to believe the lie. But I have given you this information to make a point.

I was listening to the local Christian radio station as I drove to the post office to pick up my mail one day, when I heard this woman giving her testimony. I thought this was strange but everyone who called in was telling her how wonderful it was. Let me relate her story to you and see what you think. I will call her Anna.

Now, Anna was the mother of a very rebellious 19-year-old son who I will call Ron. A very heavy drug user who had not worked a day in his life, he depended totally on what he could steal and sell and what little money his mother gave him after she paid the bills. Sometimes he would even steal money from her purse. (Well, I am wrong about him not working at all, because he sometimes sold drugs to a few of the guys he knew or to people at the parties he went to.) Ron had already been arrested several times for both drug possession and selling a controlled substance, breaking and entering, and many other crimes. Ron would never take responsibility for his actions. It was always someone else's fault he was in trouble.

Each time her son was arrested, Anna would not only bail him out but also pay for a lawyer to defend him in court. One night as Anna was getting ready for bed, the phone rang. It was a call from the local police; Ron had been arrested again, but this time it was a more serious crime. Ron had killed another man in a drug deal that had gone bad.

Anna did not have enough money to bail Ron out, so he had to stay in jail for four days while Anna tried every way she could think of to gather the money. She sold almost everything in the house, including her small collection of jewelry she had been able to accumulate and hide from Ron. She even mortgaged her home and sold her car, but she still needed $500. This she borrowed from her brother.

Once Anna and Ron were back home, they argued. Ron quickly changed cloths, and against Anna's pleading, he left to meet some friends. At 9:30 p.m. Anna's phone rang. It was the police. The officer told her he was sorry, but he had bad news. Ron had taken his friend's father's pistol from its box in the bedroom closet and committed suicide.

Well, to say the least, Anna was very distraught. She had no burial insurance on Ron. What insurance she had she had cashed in long ago. And she had sold off everything she had to get him out of jail. Some of the students held car washes to raise what money they could. Anna's family and people around town donated money. Finally, enough money was raised, and Ron was laid to rest. For two months Anna prayed and cried for him. The only thing she had to hold on to was the idea that Ron was in heaven with Jesus, which was what the preacher at her church had told her.

Late one evening Anna sat alone at the kitchen table crying in the dark when all of a sudden the room filled with light. A familiar voice spoke to her. She knew in an instant it was Ron. Before she could get over her shock, he told her he was sorry he had not been able to contact her before now but assured her he was all right. He told her that he could not stay long this time, but if she wanted him to come back, they could visit for longer periods in the future. Anna said that over the past eight months Ron has come to visit and talk at least once a week.

After listening to the story, the radio preacher's response really surprised me. Even more, the response of the listening audience almost knocked me out. Once Anna had finished her story and the host of the program began taking calls, the callers talked about how sweet it was that although he was dead Ron's thoughts were of his mother's peace of mind. There were even people calling in to see if she could somehow get Ron to deliver a message to a departed loved one of theirs. Some even said they had been to psychics several times but were still unable to get in touch with their loved ones.

The radio preacher went on and on about how God was so wonderful in the fact that he allowed Ron to contact Anna so she could have peace in her life by knowing her son was with God and there was nothing for her to worry about.

I started talking to the car radio, reminding them that this young man they were talking about had never received Jesus as His Lord and Savior, had committed murder—these two could have been rectified—and had taken his own life, which is unpardonable because in order to be forgiven for something, one has to be able to ask for forgiveness for themselves.

This is just one story in a million. The point I am trying to make is this: if God's Holy Word is telling us that the dead are still in their graves, which as I showed you, and as dead as they were when they were placed there and only our breath returns to God, then who or what is appearing to all these people claiming to be their departed loved ones?

Well, as I have shown before, these spirits are devils who are able to take on the look and mannerisms of our departed loved ones. As to going to a psychic for advice, we are told in Isaiah 8:19-20, "And when they shall say unto you, Seek unto them that have familiar spirits, and unto wizards that peep, and that mutter: should not a people seek unto their God? for the living to the dead? To the law and to the testimony: if they speak not according to this word, it is because there is no light in them."

Also, remember Luke 16:26: "And beside all this, between us and you there is a great gulf fixed: so that they which would pass from hence to you cannot; neither can they pass to us, that would come from thence." (Read the whole story in Luke 16:19-31.)

In John 11:11-14 we read the story of Lazarus. We find Jesus explaining to his disciples that Lazarus, who they knew was sick, was asleep, and they were going so Jesus could wake him. The disciples commented on how it was good for Lazarus to sleep and get his rest so he could get better. At this, knowing they had missed the point, Jesus told them plainly, "Lazarus is dead" (verse 14). (See also Leviticus 19:31 and 1 Samuel 28:8-9. There are many more verses, but these should do.) As you can plainly see, the dead are in their graves—asleep, dead—they know nothing.

In Matthew 24:24 Jesus foretold the events that will come to pass just prior to His second coming where hundreds of thousands of the elect will fall prey to many false prophets and seducing spirits that are described as "three unclean spirits like frogs" and "spirits of devils" sent from Satan himself because of the miracles they are able to perform. Since the early 1900s, this has been happening and it continues to happen today. In these latter days, the warnings of 1 Timothy 4:1 and many others are being fulfilled more than at any other time in the history of the world.

Now, in no way am I saying that no one has been risen from the dead. The Bible gives us quite a few examples of this occurring. For one, Moses was granted an early resurrection. In Jude 1:9 it says, "Yet Michael the archangel, when contending with the devil he disputed about the body of Moses, durst not bring against him a railing accusation, but said, The Lord rebuke thee." Also, we read in 2 Kings 2:9-15 about Elijah who was translated to heaven without seeing death. Both of these men appeared with our Lord Jesus Christ on the Mount of Transfiguration. (See Matthew 17:10-18.)

You see, my friend, these two men symbolize what shall occur at Jesus' second coming. The dead in Christ shall rise first; then, those who are alive shall be transformed without seeing death and shall meet Jesus in the clouds.

In Matthew 27:52-53, concerning Jesus' resurrection, we read, "And the graves were opened; and many bodies of the saints which slept arose, And came out of the graves after his resurrection, and went into the holy city, and appeared unto many."

What I am saying is, if any preacher or Bible teacher tells you he has received a new revelation, a special word of knowledge from God, has the power to heal the sick or even raise the dead, you had better be careful. Just because these people can perform what we term "miracles" does not mean the power of God is working through them. Check out *everything* he or she tells you. And I know this seems a little extreme, but we are talking about the difference between life and death.

Once I was approached by a young man about 23-years-old who was passing out Bible tracts that were promoting a large healing revival being held the following weekend. Now, I am not trying to say that I am some kind of Bible wiz, but with the help of my electronic Bible, I can hold my own on almost any level of conversation. So, when I am talking to strangers, I like to feel them out first. Not to get the upper hand on them but rather to see what level they are on so I can adjust my conversation accordingly. But, I quickly explain to them that I will not argue with them.

I could tell right away that this young man was a new convert and very eager. So, I knew that I had to choose my words carefully. I cannot explain it, but this particular young man irritated me. And I do not get irritated with people I have just met very often. I do not know if it was his approach or what, but I knew right away he was not sure of what he was saying. This is kind of how our conversation went.

Right away, he asked if I was saved and knew Jesus Christ as my Lord and Savior.

I told him I was and did.

He then asked if I had spoken in tongues or been slain in the spirit.

I told him no. Then testing him, because I knew what his next response would be, I asked him why?

He quickly opened his Bible and turned to Acts 2 and read verses 1-4.

I told him to continue reading the next eight verses.

"Why?" he asked.

I told him the next eight verses plainly showed that the apostles were not speaking gibberish, as in an unknown language as some suppose; they were speaking known languages that those around them in the crowd could understand perfectly but were unknown to the apostles themselves. Verse 11 makes this perfectly clear. It states after all the other languages are noted that "we do hear them speak in our own tongues the wonderful works of God."

As to the teaching or idea of being "slain in the spirit," from the first page of Genesis all the way to the last page of Revelation, everyone who is said to have ever been spoken to by an angel sent from heaven fell forward onto their face in adoration unless there was something right in front of them, while everyone who, as you say, is "slain in the spirit" falls to the floor on their backs. Can you tell me why this is?

He shook his head no but did not answer; so I continued.

"Look at it this way. As I said, God's true prophets, when approached by a divine being, fell forward, but look what happened to the people who came to the garden to arrest Jesus. After Jesus asked who they had come to arrest, we read in John 18:5-6, 'They answered him, Jesus of Nazareth. Jesus saith unto them, I am he. And Judas also, which betrayed him, stood with them. As soon then as he had said unto them, I am he, they went backward, and fell to the ground.'

"Now, consider this. What would happen if you hooked a wire to the negative post of your car battery then struck the other end of the wire across the positive post?"

"It would ark and sparks would fly everywhere," he answered.

"And that is exactly what John 18:5-6 is telling us. God is the positive force of the universe while Satan is the negative force. The two do not mix. One always will reject the other. It is the same with God's Word. Many preachers and Bible teachers are trying to mix Bible truths with man's traditions. They may sound good to the ear, but once you have had time to read and study God's Word, you will find that they do not mix.

"It is like all these faith healers who are suddenly appearing around the world. They come to town; set up their tents or rent a large building someplace; send out their fliers, like this one you handed me; and people flock to them, believing these men and women have been sent by God. When the people do not receive their healing, they are told by these faith healers that there must be something they have done in their lives that they have not been forgiven for; therefore, they must be out of the will of God and that is why they did not receive their healing. But if they would make a seed faith offering, God might be persuaded to change his mind, and they would receive their healing.

"This is the most ridiculous thing I have ever heard. I'm not saying there aren't people who have been healed at these places because I believe God can, will, and does heal people. What I am saying is that the healing is between God and that person who needs the healing. That man or woman standing up there on the stage running back and forth, shouting and carrying on has very little if anything to do with it. To give one example, look at what Jesus told the woman who had the blood disorder. We find her story in Matthew 9:22: 'But Jesus turned him about, and when he saw her, he said, Daughter, be of good comfort; thy faith hath made thee whole. And the woman was made whole from that hour.'

"There was no man there who had to perform some ceremony or take up a collection. Jesus himself, although the healing power flowed from Him, actually did nothing. But the point is, she had determined within herself, in verse 21, that 'if I may but touch his garment, I shall be whole.' Her faith and determination healed her. Continue reading verses 28-29.

I concluded with this thought, "There are people who will never receive a healing, not because they are bad people and God is teaching them a lesson but rather because they get impatient and give up asking God for the healing they need. One thing we must always remember is that everything happens for the glory of God. [See John 9:1-7.] We are told in the book of Job that everything has its time and God's time is not our time."

Let's turn back to our study of Revelation. In Revelation 13:15-17 we find what appears to be a little more information concerning this beast. "And he had power to give life unto the image of the beast, that the image of the beast should both speak, and cause that as many as would not worship the image of the beast should be killed. And he causeth all, both small and great, rich and poor, free and bond, to receive a mark in their right hand, or their foreheads: And that no man might buy or sell, save he that had the mark, or the name of the beast, or the number of his name."

We are also directed to a warning in Revelation 14:9-12, which states, "And the third angel followed them, saying with a loud voice, If any man worship the beast and his image, and receive his mark in his forehead, or in his hand, The same shall drink of the wine of the wrath of God, which is poured out without mixture into the cup of his indignation; and he shall be tormented with fire and brimstone in the presence of the holy angels, and in the presence of the Lamb: And the smoke of their torment ascendeth up for ever and ever: and they have no rest day nor night, who worship the beast and his image, and whosoever receiveth the mark of his name. Here is the patience of the saints: here are they that keep the commandments of God, and the faith of Jesus."

Common sense dictates that in order to have or make an image of something you must first have an original. And, as I have not only said but have also shown you proof of, who and/or what is the original beast? It can be none other than the Roman Catholic Church. As you saw, they even admit the change from the Saturday Sabbath to their Sunday Sabbath was not only an act but is a mark of their ecclesiastical power over all things religious. Anytime a church or Christian group tries to regulate how people think or what they should or should not do it is an act of aggression that sooner or later leads to persecution of others for their beliefs.

And, by the Protestant churches forming a union of church and state, we would have another ecclesiastical/civil power that would enforce religious dogmas just as the Roman Catholic Church did in her day. This is exactly what John saw in his vision of this last beast. Its nature changed from "one like a lamb" to one that "spoke as a dragon." There have been and are organizations who for years have been working to make this happen, such as the National Reform Association, the International Reform Bureau, the Lord's Day Alliance, the Federal Council of Churches of Christ, the Roman Catholic Society, the Promise Keepers, and many other splinter groups and people who are working toward this goal. I assure you that, in the very near future, these organizations, both Protestant and Roman Catholic, are destined to join hands in this common effort.

Now, think for a moment, when this happens, which of these organizations would be the ruling party? Well, of course it would be the one with the most members. And there is no doubt that the head of this alliance, simple by the numbers of their votes, would be none other than the pope.

My dear friend, in closing, let me show you one last tidbit for you to think on. This comes from the *Catholic Doctrinal Catechism.*

Q. "Have you any other way of proving that the church has power to institute festivals of precept?"

A. "Had she not such power, she could not have done that in which all modern religionist agree with, she could not have substituted the observance of Sunday, the first day of the week, for the observance of Saturday, the seventh day, a change for which there is no Scripture authority."

Q. "How prove you that the church hath power to command feast and holy days?"

A. "By the very act of changing the Sabbath into Sunday, which Protestants allow of; and therefore they fondly contradict themselves by keeping Sunday strictly, and breaking most other feast commanded by the same church. Because by keeping Sunday they acknowledge the church's power to ordain feast, and command them under sin."

I ask you, my friend, would the Catholic Church have made these statements if they were not true? I will present one more verse then leave it to you to decide. The verse is found in Revelation 18:4: "And I heard another voice from heaven, saying, Come out of her, my people, that ye be not partakers of her sins, and that ye receive not of her plagues." (Check also Isaiah 48:20.)

Now that you have read through this information, there is but one question that needs to be answered. Will you continue to worship according to man's tradition, or will you believe and worship according to God's Holy Word? I must warn you that there is not that much time left to decide. You will realize this fact as you read through the following articles.

Also, there are a couple of books that I believe every person who professes to be a Christian should read. One is *Rome's Challenge*, which asks the question, on the front page, "Why do Protestants keep Sunday?" The other is *Foxe's Book of Martyrs* written by John Fox and published by Whitaker House.

Heavenly Father, as the reader ponders on the information he or she has just read, I ask that you send the Holy Spirit near to impress on his or her mind how these truths will impact everyone's lives and how very close Your second coming really is. May they be able to get themselves ready for the hard times that are ahead. May they be able to recognize these events as they develop and unfold. As they accept Your truths, may their faith be strengthened through the times of trouble ahead. I ask this in the name of our Lord Jesus Christ, humanities only hope of salvation. Amen.

Your Brother In Christ Jesus,

Harold T. Bolieu

Book claims the pope is the devil's ally.

"Our position is that we are criticizing the system and not the individual Catholic Christians." Statement made by Richard Coffen, vice president for a Seventh-day Adventist publishing house.

Story By Jan Cienski, *Associated Press Writer.*

Richmond, Va. - Roman Catholics and some protestants are denouncing a book published by a major Protestant evangelical denomination that claims the pope is in league with the devil.

"God's Answers to Your Questions" likens the papacy to the beast in the book of Revelation, an ally of Satan in the world's final days. The Seventh-day Adventist Church publishes the book and distributes it nationally door to door.

"That the seventh head (of the beast), represents Antichrist, or the papacy, there can be little doubt," the book asserts.

The book's conclusions have no biblical basis, said Catholic clergy and lay officials and a protestant Bible scholar.

William Donohue, president of the Catholic League for Religious and Civil Rights in New York, said he often sees anti-Catholic literature, but was surprised to see it coming from a major denomination.

"For this to come from the Seventh-day Adventist and not from a splinter group, makes this offense particularly egregious," he said. "This raises the ante and makes it all the more serious."

"It's typical anti-Catholic bigotry," said Sister Mary Ann Walsh, Spokeswoman for the United States Catholic Conference.

Sibley Towner, professor of biblical interpretation at Union Theological Seminary, a Presbyterian institution in Richmond, said he was surprised the Adventist published the book. "It's outrageous and inflammatory and untrue biblically in any sense."

George Reid, head of the Biblical Research Institute of the Seventh-day Adventist Church, said the book merely follows the lead of such Protestant Reformers as Martin Luther and John Calvin.

"We still believe that it's the reasonable way to understand these prophesies, arising from the text itself and not political correctness," he said.

The Seventh-day Adventist Church is based in Silver Spring, Md., and traces its origins to William Miller of New Hampton, N.Y., who predicted that the world would end in the 1840's. The Church says it has 9 million members worldwide.

The book is published by the Review and Herald Publishing Association in Hagertown, MD., one of the denomination's main publishing houses.

Richard Coffen, vice president for editorial services at the publishing house, said he did not know how many copies of the book had been distributed.

Coffen said the book was a critique, not bigotry, and that

it attacks the papacy, not specific popes. "Our position is that we are criticizing the system and not individual Catholic Christians."

Donohue said he has heard that argument before. "It's like saying to children, 'I hate your father and I hate your mother, but I don't hate you.'"

The book says those who follow papal teachings are Satan's allies.

"Those who acknowledge the supremacy of the beast by yielding obedience to the law of God as changed and enforced by the papacy, worship the beast. Such will take the side of Satan in his rebellion against God's authority," the book says.

Linking the pope to the Antichrist springs from the days of the reformation 500 years ago when new Protestant churches were battling Roman Catholics, Towner. "In the Reformation, Protestants threw the word Antichrist around a lot," he said. "But that has not been done in mainliune Protestant circles for centuries."

Anti-Catholic language these days usually comes from small sectarian groups affiliated with right-wing political causes such as the Ku Klux Klan, Towner said.

The book comes at a time when relations between evangelical Christians and Catholics have been improving. In 1994, Southern Baptist, the country's largest Protestant denomination, and the Catholic Church endorsed a dialogue between the two denominations.

The Christian Coalition also has been trying to build ties to socially conservative Catholics.

"There have been a number of attempts to build political

coalitions between Catholics and conservative Protestants," said William Dinges, professor of religious studies at the Catholic University of America in Washington. "Conservative Catholics who would move to the right on cultural issues might be offended by this."

Donohue said he doubts the book will influence anyone, but it concerns him nonetheless.

"This kind of anti-Catholicism cannot be discounted," he said. "It's affecting the Joe Sixpacks of this world, and these people are not unimportant and it has to be taken seriously."

Vatican Thinking Evolves

The Pope Gives His Blessing To Natural Selection, Through Man's Soul Remains Beyond Science's Reach. Augustinian: John Paul Does Not Interpret The Bible Literally.

The relationship between faith and science can be vexing, but one way the Roman Catholic Church and mainstream Protestant denominations reconcile the two is to say they each deal with different spheres of knowledge and so are not in conflict. This is a sort of metaphysical version of Christ admonition to render to Caesar what is Caesar's and to God what is God's, and it is position that Pope John Paul II reaffirmed last week when he made a statement on evolution. "Consideration of the method used in diverse orders of knowledge allows for the concordance of two points of view which seem irreconcil-able," he wrote. "The sciences of observation describe and measure with ever greater precision the multi-ple manifestations of life, while theology extracts the final meaning according to the Creator's designs."

In his message to a meeting of the Pontifical Academy of Sciences, which had taken the origin of life as its theme.

John Paul described the shift in the church's view of evolution that has taken place since Pope Pius XII issued his encyclical Humani Generis in 1950. "Humani Generis," John Paul wrote, "considered the doctrine of evolutionism as a serious hypothesis, worthy of a more deeply studied investigation. Today, new knowledge leads us to recognize that the theory of evolution is more than hypothesis

You will find the entire story in Time, November 4, 1996.

Written By James Collins, Reported by Greg Burke/ Rome and Ratu Kamlani/New York.

THE POPE AND DARWIN.

"The Pope Says We May Descend From Monkeys."

Did God create mankind in his image, as the Bible says, or did humans evolve from animals, as Darwin theorized nearly 150 years ago? According to Pope John Paul II, evolution may be the better explanation. Weighing in on a debate that has divided Christians for decades, the pope declared that evolution is "more than just a theory" and is fully compatible with the Christian faith," he stated in a letter to the Pontifical Academy of Sciences. You will find the entire story in U.Snews and Report, November 4, 1996.

Written by Jeffery L. Sheler.

NO FORGIVENESS 'DIRECTLY FROM GOD' POPE SAYS.

VATICAN CITY - Rebutting a belief widely shared by Protestants and a growing number of Roman Catholics, Pope John Paul II on Tuesday dismissed the "wide-spread idea that one can obtain forgiveness directly from God" and exhorted Catholics to confess more often to their priest.

The pontiff issued a major document calling for "the restoration of a proper sense of sin" in a world "shattered to its very foundation" by evils ranging from social discrimination to nuclear stockpiling.

Officially called an "apostolic exhortation," the 138 - page papal document focuses on the sacrament of reconciliation and penance, informally known as confession - an obligation of all Catholics that has increasingly fallen into disuse, especially in the industrial countries.

Changing life styles, particularly in advanced countries such as the United States, have led some priest to administer "general absolution" of whole congregations instead of hearing traditional individual confessions.

But the Pope warned against that trend, saying, "This form cannot become an ordinary one." The papal document said general absolution can be applicable only in special circumstances or in places where there is no permanent priest. "Confession of sins must ordinarily be individual and not collective, just as sin is a deeply personal matter," the papal document said. Written By Don A. Schanche, Times Staff Writer, Wednesday, December 12, 1984, Part 1, page 11.

In a related story, Pope John Paul II's decision to set aside a special year devoted to Mary reflects his desire to bring back such traditional customs as pilgrimages to sanctuaries and religious processions. Vatican officials say. The Vatican said that Catholics could gain indulgence, or the pardon of temporal punishment of sin, by devoutly taking part in some of the Marian year activities. From the outset of his pontificate more than eight years ago, John Paul has displayed special devotion to her. He calls Mary the 'heavenly mother of the church' and often invokes her intercession in public prayers. This story is from the Associated Press, dated February 17, 1987.

You may find this next story kind-of confusing because the writer (although Sunday is mentioned as a day of rest), does not make plain if he is talking about the Catholic Sabbath, which is Sunday, the first day of the week, or the Bible Sabbath, which is Saturday, the seventh day of the week. To prove this to yourself simply go to the library and check the Catholic Catechism book and look up the Sabbath Day. But the article begins with a statement as its heading, then he ask a question.

Disregarding Sunday As Day Of Rest May Hurt Us Culturally.

Is killing Sunday killing us? "The current trend toward destroying Sunday as a day of rest may indicate that in our civilization something is rotten at the core," says an editorial in a Lutheran magazine. "Our whole physical, mental and spiritual well-being seems to demand a time when the community is at rest and the pressures of life are lifted." If this is so important, why isn't the writer of the editorial named?

"Movement to reclaim Sabbath grows," reads a newspaper headline for a story about the Lord's Day Alliance, an interdenominational group that wants to protect the Sabbath. Again, if this is so important, then why isn't the writer who wrote the headline named? In fact there is only one name throughout the entire piece, and that name is of the Catholic Pope Himself, Pope John Paul II. We are informed, "It is the churches that are showing the most concern about the neglect of Sunday. Pope John Paul II, in a strongly worded, 100-page apostolic letter in June, reminded the world's Catholics of their obligation to "sanctify the holy day" by attending Mass regularly on Sunday Now my question is simple. Why would Protestants want to follow what the Catholic Pope says? After all, it was the Catholic Churches early leaders who changed their Sabbath Day to Sunday in order to separate themselves from all the Protestant Churches, then after a time tried to force everyone else to go along with that change. This story was written by George R. Plagenz, and syndicated by the Newspaper Enterprise Association. No date given.

FOLLOWING ARE IDENTIFYING FACTS OF THE LITTLE HORN OF DANIEL 13:15-17.

Only Through God's Holy Word Can We Prove That It Is A Man, Not A Machine, We Are Looking For.
"and behold, in this horn were eyes like the eyes of a man, and a mouth speaking great things."
Daniel 7:8, bottom section.

"And that no man might buy sell, save he that had the MARK, or the NAME of the BEAST, or the NUMBER of HIS NAME.. Here is wisdom, let him that hath understanding count the number of the beast: for it is the number of a man; and HIS NUMBER is SIX HUNDRED and THREE-SCORE and SIX.
(OR 666.) Revelation 13:17-18.

Back in the seventeenth century, before this coded mystery was unraveled, every Popes title was found written on the three tier crown which each New Pope received after being Ordained. This title is VICARIUS FILII DEI, which is Latin for VICAR OF THE SON OF GOD. Catholic's are taught from a very young age that the church, which is a visible society, and must have a visible head. Hence to the Bishop of Rome, as Head of the Church, was given the title of VICAR OF CHRIST." Our Sunday Visitor, a Catholic Weekly, Bureau of information, Huntington, Ind., April 18,1915.

"The numeral letters of His Name shall make up this number.666 "The Douay (Catholic Bible), note on Revelation 13:18.

"The method generally adopted is that known as the Ghematria of the rabbins, which assigns each letter of a name its usual numerical value, and gives the sum of such numbers as the equivalent of the Name." Marvin R. Vincent, D.D., Word Studies in the New Testament, Notes on Revelation 13:18.

"Reason and sense demand the acceptance of one or the other of these alternatives; either Protestantism and keeping holy of Saturday, or Catholicity and keeping holy of Sunday. Compromise is impossible." The Catholic Mirror, December 23, 1893.

"Now we challenge the world to find another name in these three languages: Greek, Hebrew, and Latin

Which shall designate the same numbers. See John 19:20, which states, "This title then read many of the Jews: for the place where Jesus was crucified was nigh to the city: and it was written in Hebrew, Greek, and Latin."

"Let no man deceive you by any means: for that day shall not come, except there come a falling away first, and that man of sin be revealed, the son of perdition; Who opposeth and exalteth himself above all that is called God, or that is worshipped; so that he as God sitteth in the temple of God, shewing himself that he is God." II Thessalonians 2:3-4.

"The Pope is of so great dignity and so exalted that he is not a mere man, but as it were God, and the Vicar Of God." "The Pope is of such lofty and supreme dignity that, properly speaking, he has not been established in any rank of dignity, but rather has been placed upon the very summit of all ranks of dignities." "He is likewise the divine monarch and supreme emperor and king of kings." "Hence the Pope is crowned with a triple crown, as King of Heaven and of the Earth and of the Lower Regions." Lucius Ferraris, Prompta Bibliotheca (Catholic Dictionary), Vol. VI, pgs. 438, 442.

"The observance of Sunday by the Protestants is an Homage they pay in spite of themselves to the authority of the Catholic Church." Monsignor Louis Segur, Plain Talk about Protestantism of today, pg. 213.

"Of course the Catholic Church claims that the change (of worshiping on Sunday, the first day of the week, instead of Saturday as instructed by God), was her act, and this act is a Mark of her Ecclesiastical Authority in religious things." H.F. Thomas, Chancellor of Cardinal Gibbons.

INDEX OF REFERENCES LISTED IN SEQUENCE BY PAGE NUMBER.

www.ingramcontent.com/pod-product-compliance
Lightning Source LLC
Chambersburg PA
CBHW060544100426
42742CB00013B/2444